"THOREAU," wrote Mr. Teale in the introduction to his edition of *Walden,* "was not only a revolutionary and original thinker, but a great craftsman whose trade was sentences . . . sentences that condensed thoughts into brilliant epigrams, that soared into the realm of pure poetry . . ."

On the centenary of Thoreau's death, Mr. Teale has collected from the several books of Thoreau and from his extensive journal the most striking of these memorable passages on nature, writing, truth, man's future, birds, stars, etc. In these pages is made available the essence of Thoreau's genius, with biographical comments by America's foremost living naturalist-writer.

Edwin Way Teale, a past president of The Thoreau Society, has edited and illustrated an annotated edition of *Walden* which is now available in the Great Illustrated Classics published by Dodd, Mead & Company.

The Thoughts of Thoreau

CONTENTS

Contents

THE THOUGHTS
OF THOREAU

Thoreau

Selected with a Biographical Foreword
and Introduction by

Edwin Way Teale

D O D D , M E A D & C O M P A N Y - New York

NOTE: *In some instances Thoreau's punctuation has been simplified as, for example, where he uses both a comma and a dash the comma has been omitted as unnecessary. Occasionally, in order to include the widest possible variety of Thoreau's thoughts in the space available, phrases or sentences that are extraneous or do not contribute directly to the idea have been omitted. In the interests of appearance, such omissions have not been indicated. But nothing has been omitted that would in any way alter or qualify Thoreau's thought.* E.W.T.

PRINTED IN THE UNITED STATES OF AMERICA
BY VAIL-BALLOU PRESS, INC., BINGHAMTON, N.Y.

Biographical Foreword

Henry David Thoreau was born, on July 12, 1817, at Concord, Massachusetts, that fertile seed-bed in which so much of lasting importance developed. There he lived and there he died on May 6, 1862.

Of all the noted men of letters whose names are associated with Concord—Emerson, Alcott, Hawthorne, Thoreau—he, alone, was born there. Christened David Henry by his parents, John and Cynthia Dunbar Thoreau, he transposed these given names early in manhood. Thereafter he signed his name: Henry D. Thoreau.

During his life-span of fewer than forty-five years, he was graduated from Harvard, taught school, lectured, made pencils, acted as caretaker at Ralph Waldo Emerson's, did surveying and manual labor. By simplifying his life and reducing his expenditures, he calculated that about six weeks of work were sufficient to support him throughout the year. This left him free during most of his time to follow his own individual way of life, rambling over the countryside and setting down his thoughts. On October 22, 1837, at the age of twenty, Thoreau made the first entry in his *Journal*. It was the great continuing book of his life that grew to at least forty manuscript volumes.

In 1839, accompanied by his older brother, John, Thoreau journeyed in a homemade rowboat on the Concord and Merrimack Rivers, ascending the latter stream above Manchester, N.H. Aside from this trip, excursions to Cape Cod, the Maine Woods and the White Mountains, and part of one year tutoring in the family of Emerson's brother, William, on Staten Island, Thoreau spent most of his life ruminating amid the same Concord scenes, recording in his *Journal* his thoughts and observations.

The most dramatic event of Thoreau's years occurred on Independence Day, 1845. On that Fourth of July, he moved to a hut he had built on land owned by Emerson, on the shore of Walden Pond, a mile and a half south of Concord. There he lived alone for more than two years, until September 6, 1847. There he wrote his first book, *A Week on the Concord and Merrimack Rivers*, and there he collected material for his masterpiece, *Walden; or Life in the Woods*. So unsuccessful was *The Week*, published in 1849, that four years later fewer than 300 copies had been sold of the 1000 that had been published at Thoreau's expense. However, *Walden*, issued by Ticknor and Fields in 1854, immediately attracted a circle of admirers that has continued to expand. The book has appeared in more than 100 editions. It has been translated into virtually all modern languages.

While Thoreau was living beside the pond, he was

arrested and spent a night in jail for refusing to pay his poll tax to a state that supported slavery. His later essay, *Civil Disobedience,* represents an important milestone on the road toward social progress. It has provided a guide for minority groups in many parts of the world. Translated by Mahatma Gandhi, it inspired the passive resistance movement in India. During the period of John Brown's trial and execution, just before the Civil War, Thoreau was one of his most eloquent defenders.

When he was forty-three, in 1860, he contracted bronchitis which developed into tuberculosis. The following summer he journeyed to Minnesota for his health but returned unimproved. He died the following May at the age of forty-four years, nine months and twenty-four days.

Few men of accomplishment have enjoyed so wide a margin of leisure in their lives as Henry Thoreau. Few have had the supreme courage and self-confidence to walk, as he did, alone. The world has had to take him on his own terms. That it has is indicated by the fact that in New York City, on May 6, 1962, a century to a day after his death, his bust was unveiled at the Hall of Fame for Great Americans.

Introduction

One June day, nearly forty years ago, I set out in a row-boat with a companion to follow the Ohio River for 400 miles from Louisville, Kentucky, to the Mississippi. At the end of the second day my friend recalled some pressing matter that took him elsewhere and I continued rowing alone for the remaining 330 miles.

Somewhere along the way I stopped at a small river town whose name I cannot remember. On a dusty table in a hole-in-the-wall bookshop I came upon a pocket-sized volume of extracts from the writings of Henry David Thoreau. In the days that followed, I would pull out into the middle of the stream and let the boat ride with the current for half an hour at a time, reading as I drifted.

It was under such circumstances that I came upon a paragraph that often returned to my mind in succeeding years. The sentences were from a letter by Thoreau to his Worcester friend, Harrison Blake:

"I have just put another stick into my stove . . . I

suppose I have burned up a pretty good-sized tree to-night—and for what? I settled with Mr. Tarbell for it the other day; but that wasn't the final settlement. I got off cheaply from him. At last, one will say, 'Let me see, how much wood did you burn, Sir?' And I shall shudder to think that the next question will be, 'What did you do while you were warm?' "

Those words were set down on December 19, 1854, four months and ten days after the publication of *Walden.* They reflect that lifelong concern for time and man's use of time that is ever-present in the writings of Thoreau. For him, the highest employment of time was in the capture of his thoughts. He fished in the stream of time for thoughts. He set his traps in the fields and woods for thoughts. "Our thoughts," he wrote in his *Journal* in 1850, "are the epochs of our life: all else is but as a journal of the winds that blew while we were here."

It was Thoreau's habit to make "minutes" of his ideas and observations while on his solitary rambles. These he later entered, often in expanded form, in his *Journal.* From this immense repository of his thoughts he mined the blocks which he fitted together to form the two books published during his lifetime. In the first, *A Week on the Concord and Merrimack Rivers,* his thoughts are held together by the narrative of a rowboat trip made in 1839 with his brother, John; in the second, *Walden,* by the story of his two years in the hut beside Deep Cove. It was this adventure in living that dramatized his outlook as a poet-naturalist, a rebel and a moral philosopher.

Although he did surveying, made pencils and engaged in manual labor, his main occupation throughout his life was thinking and expressing his thoughts on paper. His ideas are always stimulating. To some they seem penetrating truths; to others, on occasion, perverse and outrageous opinions. But always they are driving home what Thoreau conceived to be the most important considerations of life. They are written to catch the attention of wandering minds, to goad his fellowmen into seriousness.

Running through all of Thoreau's writings, running all through his life, is the intensity of his feeling for nature, for wildness. To few people in the world has nature meant so much as it did to Thoreau. For an increasing number of city-men, whose background ill fits them to appreciate his viewpoint, this phase of Thoreau's writings may be more baffling than his paradoxes.

In the decades following his death, there was a tendency to view him as a nature writer mainly or even merely. His philosophical and economic views were considered, as one writer of the time put it, "not much." This estimate, rightly, has changed. But in stressing his importance in the realms of philosophy and politics and economics, a disposition has grown on the part of some to dismiss his pages on nature as of small consequence.

Yet the bulk of the thousands of pages of his *Journal* is devoted to entries on nature and natural history. Thoreau was a pioneer in the field of limnology. A century ahead of his time, he expressed modern ideas on conservation and forestry and the preservation of wild lands. He was many-sided; all facets should share in our attention. To ignore or dismiss the importance of Thoreau's deep involvement with nature is to separate him from the very fountainhead of his inspiration.

Although Thoreau was capable of writing so supreme an example of the awkward sentence as: "I saw in Stowe some trees fuller of apples still than I remember to have seen," in the main he expressed his thoughts with brilliant clarity and memorable succinctness, compressing his ideas into such lines as: "Nothing is so much to be feared as fear," "We live but a fraction of our life" and "A man sits as many risks as he runs." Such a collection as this volume, drawn from his many pages, reveals Thoreau's range and stature as one of the great aphorists of the world.

Occasionally the too-literal minded will be puzzled. And often the fast reader, accustomed to gulping down pages at a time, will have to stay his haste, return and chew longer on some of the gnarled and concentrated paragraphs of Thoreau. But those who read perceptively will find, time after time, that his sentences open like windows on a wider prospect of thought.

A hundred years have passed since Henry Thoreau died on a May morning in 1862. All during the intervening century, the world has been hurrying away from the ideas he expressed. It has moved away from simplicity toward complexity, away from the country to the city, away from nature toward a man-made environment, away from individual and inner responsibility toward external control.

Why, then, are the thoughts of Thoreau of any importance? Why has interest in his life and philosophy grown with the years? What does Thoreau have to say to modern man?

The problems he dealt with have not been altered by the passing of a century. For they concern mind and spirit, character and personality, man's integrity and his ideals, the uses of time and the purposes of life. Thoreau is always calling the attention of men—who delight in fighting far from home—to battles still unfought within themselves. He is an abolitionist whose concern is not the abolition of Negro slavery merely but the ending of slavery of all kinds, in all times. He speaks for the improvement of men—which has been slow—rather than the improvement of things—which has been swift. While the world is intent on increasing the efficiency of means, Thoreau emphasizes also the necessity of improving the ends.

In such incisive sentences as: "Men have become the tools of their tools," he states the increasing dilemma of modern man. With satellites and intercontinental rockets and atomic bombs culminating a century of scientific progress, we feel more tense, more insecure, because our means to unimproved ends have been so awesomely advanced. In such a time, the thoughts of Thoreau have gained, rather than lost, in pertinency.

EDWIN WAY TEALE

Trail Wood,
Hampton, Connecticut

On Himself ✍ ✍

✍ If I am not I, who will be?

JOURNAL, *August 9, 1841.*

✍ I would rather sit on a pumpkin and have it all to myself than be crowded on a velvet cushion.

WALDEN, *Chapter I.*

✍ I should not talk so much about myself if there were anybody else whom I knew as well.

WALDEN, *Chapter I.*

✍ My greatest skill has been to want but little.

JOURNAL, *July 19, 1851.*

✍ I cannot tell you what I am, more than a ray of the summer's sun. What I am I am, and say not. Being is the great explainer.

JOURNAL, *February 26, 1841.*

🖋 I only know myself as a human entity, the scene, so to speak, of thoughts and affections, and am sensible of a certain doubleness by which I stand as remote from myself as from another. However intense my experience, I am conscious of the presence and criticism of a part of me which, as it were, is not a part of me, but spectator, sharing no experience, but taking note of it, and that is no more I than it is you. When the play—it may be the tragedy of life—is over, the spectator goes his way. It was a kind of fiction, a work of the imagination only, so far as he was concerned. A man *may* be affected by a theatrical exhibition; on the other hand, he *may not* be affected by an actual event which appears to concern him never so much.

JOURNAL, August 8, 1852.

🖋 I came into this world, not chiefly to make this a good place to live in, but to live in it, be it good or bad.

CIVIL DISOBEDIENCE.

🖋 I long ago lost a hound, a bay horse, and a turtle-dove, and am still on their trail. Many are the travelers I have spoken concerning them, describing their tracks and what calls they answered to. I have met one or two who have heard the hound, and the tramp of the horse, and even seen the dove disappear behind a cloud, and they seemed as anxious to recover them as if they had lost them themselves.

WALDEN, Chapter I.

🖋 How alone must our life be lived! We dwell on the seashore, and none between us and the sea. Men are my merry companions, my fellow-pilgrims, who beguile the way but leave me at the first turn of the road, for none are travelling *one* road so far as myself.

JOURNAL, March 13, 1841.

I was not born to be forced. I will breathe after my own fashion.

CIVIL DISOBEDIENCE.

My Aunt Maria asked me to read the life of Dr. Chalmers, which however I did not promise to do. Yesterday, Sunday, she was heard through the partition shouting to my Aunt Jane, who is deaf, "Think of it! He stood half an hour today to hear the frogs croak, and he wouldn't read the life of Chalmers."

JOURNAL, March 28, 1853.

If my curve is large, why bend it to a smaller circle?

JOURNAL, July 19, 1851.

I am grateful for what I am and have. My thanksgiving is perpetual. It is surprising how contented one can be with nothing definite—only a sense of existence.

LETTER TO HARRISON BLAKE, December 6, 1856.

In youth, before I lost any of my senses, I can remember that I was all alive, and inhabited my body with inexpressible satisfaction; both its weariness and its refreshment were sweet to me. This earth was the most glorious musical instrument, and I was audience to its strains.

JOURNAL, July 16, 1851.

🖋 One day a man came to my hut from Lexington to inquire after his hound that made a large track, and had been hunting for a week by himself. But I fear that he was not the wiser for all I told him, for every time I attempted to answer his questions he interrupted me by asking, "What do you do here?" He had lost a dog, but found a man.

WALDEN, Chapter XV.

🖋 I have never got over my surprise that I should have been born into the most estimable place in all the world, and in the very nick of time, too.

JOURNAL, December 5, 1856.

🖋 I have a real genius for staying at home.

LETTER TO DANIEL RICKETSON, February 1, 1855.

🖋 I have traveled a good deal in Concord.

WALDEN, Chapter I.

🖋 I cut another furrow than you see. Where the off ox treads, there it is not, it is farther off; where the nigh ox walks, it will not be, it is nigher still.

JOURNAL, April 7, 1841.

🖋 Ah, that life that I have known! How hard it is to remember what is most memorable! We remember how we itched, not how our hearts beat.

JOURNAL, June 11, 1851.

🖋 I went to the woods because I wished to live deliberately, to front only the essential facts of life, and see if I could learn what it had to teach, and not, when I came to die, discover that I had not lived. I did not wish to live what was not life, living is so dear; nor did I wish to practice resignation, unless it was quite necessary. I wanted to live deep and suck out all the marrow of life, to live so sturdily and Spartan-like as to put to rout all that was not life, to cut a broad swath and shave close, to drive life into a corner, and reduce it to its lowest terms, and, if it proved to be mean, why then to get the whole and genuine meanness of it, and publish its meanness to the world; or if it were sublime, to know it by experience, and be able to give a true account of it in my next excursion.

WALDEN, Chapter II.

Alcott spent the day with me yesterday. He spent the day before with Emerson. He observed that he had got his wine and now he had come after his venison.

JOURNAL, August 10, 1858.

I remember how glad I was when I was kept from school a half a day to pick huckleberries on a neighboring hill all by myself to make a pudding for the family dinner. Ah, they got nothing but the pudding, but I got invaluable experience beside! A half a day of liberty like that was the promise of life eternal. It was emancipation in New England. O, what a day was there, my countrymen!

JOURNAL, July 16, 1851.

✍ I did not wish to take a cabin passage, but rather to go before the mast and on the deck of the world, for there I could best see the moonlight amid the mountains. I do not wish to go below now.

WALDEN, Chapter XVIII.

✍ Methinks my seasons revolve more slowly than those of nature; I am differently timed.

JOURNAL, July 19, 1851.

✍ Here I am thirty-four years old, and yet my life is almost wholly unexpanded. How much is in the germ! There is such an interval between my ideal and the actual in many instances that I may say I am unborn.

JOURNAL, July 19, 1851.

✍ The greater part of what my neighbors call good I believe in my soul to be bad, and if I repent of anything it is very likely to be my good behavior.

WALDEN, Chapter I.

✍ I feel slightly complimented when Nature condescends to make use of me without my knowledge, as when I help scatter her seeds in my walk, or carry burs and cockles on my clothes from field to field. I feel as though I had done something for the commonweal, and were entitled to board and lodging. I take such airs upon me as the boy who holds a horse for the circus company, whom all the spectators envy.

JOURNAL, February 6, 1841.

✍ I believe in the forest, and in the meadow, and in the night in which the corn grows.

WALKING.

✍ I had three chairs in my house; one for solitude, two for friendship, three for society.

WALDEN, Chapter VI.

✍ From time to time I overlook the promised land, but I do not feel that I am travelling toward it.

JOURNAL, 1850.

✍ I enjoy more drinking water at a clear spring than out of a goblet at a gentleman's table. I like best the bread which I have baked, the garment which I have made, the shelter which I have constructed, the fuel which I have gathered.

JOURNAL, October 20, 1855.

✍ For sympathy with my neighbors I might about as well live in China. They are to me barbarians, with their committee-works and gregariousness.

JOURNAL, October 29, 1855.

✍ Society, man, has no prize to offer me that can tempt me; not one. That which interests a town or city or any large number of men is always something trivial, as politics. It is impossible for me to be interested in what interests men generally. Their pursuits and interests seem to me frivolous. When I am most myself and see the clearest, men are least to be seen.

JOURNAL, April 24, 1852.

✍ One young man of my acquaintance, who has inherited some acres, told me that he thought he should live as I did, *if he had the means.* I would not have any one adopt *my* mode of living on any account; for, beside that before he has fairly learned it I may have found out another for myself, I desire that there may be as many different persons in the world as possible; but I would have each one be very careful to find out and pursue *his own* way, and not his father's or his mother's or his neighbor's instead.

WALDEN, Chapter I.

✍ My excuse for not lecturing against the use of tobacco is, that I never chewed it, that is the penalty which reformed tobacco-chewers have to pay; though there are things enough I have chewed which I could lecture against.

WALDEN, Chapter I.

✍ Perhaps the facts most astounding and most real are never communicated by man to man. The true harvest of my daily life is somewhat as intangible and indescribable as the tints of morning or evening. It is a little star-dust caught, a segment of the rainbow which I have clutched.

WALDEN, Chapter XI.

✍ I feel that my life is very homely, my pleasures very cheap. Joy and sorrow, success and failure, grandeur and meanness, and indeed most of the words in the English language do not mean for me what they do for my neighbors. I see that my neighbors look with compassion on me, that they think it is a mean and unfortunate destiny which makes me walk in these fields and woods so much and sail on this river alone. But so long as I find here the only real elysium, I cannot hesitate in my choice.

JOURNAL, October 18, 1856.

🖎 I do not propose to write an ode to dejection, but to brag as lustily as chanticleer in the morning, standing on his roost, if only to wake my neighbors up.

WALDEN, Chapter II.

🖎 For a year or two past, my *publisher*, falsely so called, has been writing from time to time to ask what disposition should be made of the copies of "A Week on the Concord and Merrimack Rivers" still on hand, and at last suggesting that he had use for the room they occupied in his cellar. So I had them all sent to me here, and they have arrived today by express, filling the man's wagon—706 copies out of an edition of 1000 which I bought of Munroe four years ago and have been ever since paying for, and have not quite paid for yet. I now have a library of nearly nine hundred volumes, over seven hundred of which I wrote myself. Nevertheless, in spite of this result, sitting beside the inert mass of my works, I take up my pen tonight to record what thought or experience I have had, with as much satisfaction as ever. Indeed, I believe that this result is more inspiring and better for me than if a thousand had bought my wares. It affects my privacy less and leaves me freer.

JOURNAL, October 28, 1853.

By poverty, i.e. simplicity of life and fewness of incidents, I am solidified and crystallized, as a vapor or liquid by cold.

JOURNAL, *February 8, 1857.*

I am disappointed to find that most that I am and value myself for is lost, or worse than lost, on my audience. I fail to get even the attention of the mass. I should suit them better if I suited myself less. I feel that the public demand an average man—average thoughts and manners—not originality, nor even absolute excellence. You cannot interest them except as you are like them and sympathize with them. I would rather that my audience come to me than that I should go to them, and so they be sifted; i.e., I would rather write books than lectures.

JOURNAL, *December 6, 1854.*

I am from time to time congratulating myself on my general want of success as a lecturer; apparent want of success, but is it not a real triumph? I do my work clean as I go along, and they will not be likely to want me anywhere again.

LETTER TO THOMAS CHOLMONDELEY, *February 7, 1855.*

For many years I was self-appointed inspector of snow-storms and rain-storms, and did my duty faithfully, though I never received one cent for it.

JOURNAL, *1845–47.*

I sit in my boat on Walden, playing the flute this evening, and see the perch, which I seem to have charmed, hovering around me, and the moon travelling over the bottom, which is strewn with the wrecks of the forest, and feel that nothing but the wildest imagination can conceive of the manner of life we are living. Nature is the wizard. The Concord nights are stranger than the Arabian nights.

JOURNAL, May 27, 1841.

In the street and in society I am almost invariably cheap and dissipated, my life is unspeakably mean. No amount of gold or respectability would in the least redeem it—dining with the Governor or a member of Congress! But alone in distant woods or fields, in unpretending sprout-lands or pastures tracked by rabbits, even in a bleak and, to most, cheerless day, like this, when a villager would be thinking of his inn, I come to myself, I once more feel myself grandly related, and that cold and solitude are friends of mine. I suppose that this value, in my case, is equivalent to what others get by churchgoing and prayer. I come to my solitary woodland walk as the homesick go home.

JOURNAL, January 7, 1857.

I think I cannot preserve my health and spirits, unless I spend four hours a day at least—and it is commonly more than that—sauntering through the woods and over the hills and fields, absolutely free from all worldly engagements.

WALKING.

🖊 I am so wedded to my way of spending a day—require such broad margins of leisure, and such a complete wardrobe of old clothes, that I am ill-fitted for going abroad. Pleasant is it sometimes to sit at home, on a single egg all day, in your own nest, though it may prove at last to be an egg of chalk. The old coat that I wear is Concord; it is my morning-robe and my study-gown, my working dress and suit of ceremony, and my nightgown after all. Cleave to the simplest ever. Home—home—home. *Cars* sound like *cares* to me.

LETTER TO DANIEL RICKETSON, September 27, 1855.

🖊 We must go out and re-ally ourselves to Nature every day. We must take root, and send out some little fibre at least, even every winter day. I am sensible that I am imbibing health when I open my mouth to the wind. Staying in the house breeds a sort of insanity always. Every house is in this sense a hospital. A night and a forenoon is as much confinement to those wards as I can stand. I am aware that I recover some sanity which I had lost almost the instant that I come abroad.

JOURNAL, December 29, 1856.

🖊 I omit the unusual—the hurricanes and earthquakes—and describe the common. This has the greatest charm and is the true theme of poetry. You may have the extraordinary for your province, if you will let me have the ordinary.

JOURNAL, August 28, 1851.

I am always gathering my crop from these woods and fields and waters, and no man is in my way or interferes with me. My crop is not their crop. Today I see them gathering in their beans and corn, and they are a spectacle to me, but are soon out of my sight. I am not gathering beans and corn. Do they think there are no fruits but such as these? I am a reaper; I am not a gleaner. I go reaping, cutting as broad a swath as I can, and bundling and stacking up and carrying it off from field to field, and no man knows nor cares. My crop is not sorghum nor Davis seedlings. There are other crops than these, whose seed is not distributed by the Patent Office.

JOURNAL, October 14, 1857.

I make it my business to extract from Nature whatever nutriment she can furnish me, though at the risk of endless iteration. I milk the sky and the earth.

JOURNAL, November 3, 1853.

I spend the forenoon in my chamber, writing or arranging my papers, and in the afternoon I walk forth into the fields and woods. I turn aside, perchance, into some withdrawn, untrodden swamp, and find these bilberries, large and fair, awaiting me in inexhaustible abundance, for I have no tame garden.

JOURNAL, August 9, 1853.

Again and again I congratulate myself on my so-called poverty. I was almost disappointed yesterday to find thirty dollars in my desk which I did not know that I possessed, though now I should be sorry to lose it. The week that I go away to lecture, however much I may get from it, is unspeakably cheapened. The preceding and succeeding days are a mere sloping down and up from it.

JOURNAL, February 8, 1857.

✍ How to extract its honey from the flower of the world. That is my everyday business. I am as busy as a bee about it. I ramble over all fields on that errand, and am never so happy as when I feel myself heavy with honey and wax. I am like a bee searching the livelong day for the sweets of nature.

JOURNAL, September 7, 1851.

✍ If anybody else—any farmer, at least—should spend an hour thus wading about here in this secluded swamp, barelegged, intent on the sphagnum, filling his pockets only, with no rake in his hand and no bag or bushel on the bank, he would be pronounced insane and have a guardian put over him; but if he'll spend his time skimming and watering his milk and selling his small potatoes for large ones, or generally skinning flints, he will probably be made guardian of somebody else.

JOURNAL, August 30, 1856.

✍ For years I marched to a music in comparison with which the military music of the streets is noise and discord. I was daily intoxicated, and yet no man could call me intemperate. With all your science can you tell how it is, and whence it is, that light comes into the soul?

JOURNAL, July 16, 1851.

How many fine thoughts has every man had! How few fine thoughts are expressed! Yet we never have a fantasy so subtle and ethereal, but that *talent merely*, with more resolution and faithful persistency, after a thousand failures, might fix and engrave it in distinct and enduring words, and we should see that our dreams are the solidest facts that we know.

LETTER TO HARRISON BLAKE, March 27, 1848.

Somebody shut the cat's tail in the door just now, and she made such a caterwaul as has driven two whole worlds out of my thoughts. I saw unspeakable things in the sky and looming in the horizon of my mind, and now they are all reduced to a cat's tail.

JOURNAL, November 16, 1850.

I would fain keep a journal which should contain those thoughts and impressions which I am most liable to forget that I have had; which would have in one sense the greatest remoteness, in another, the greatest nearness to me.

JOURNAL, 1851.

A wakeful night will yield as much thought as a long journey. If I try thoughts by their quality, not their quantity, I may find that a restless night will yield more than the longest journey.

JOURNAL, January 30, 1852.

The pleasures of the intellect are permanent, the pleasures of the heart are transitory.

JOURNAL, January 22, 1852.

I have been making pencils all day, and then at evening walked to see an old school-mate who is going to help make the Welland Canal navigable for ships around Niagara. He cannot see any such motives and modes of living as I; professes not to look beyond the securing of certain "creature comforts." And so we go silently different ways, with all sincerity, I in the still moonlight through the village this fair evening to write these thoughts in my journal, and he, forsooth, to mature his schemes to ends as good, maybe, but different. So are we two made, while the same stars shine quietly over us. If I or he be wrong, Nature yet consents placidly. She bites her lips and smiles to see how her children will agree. So does the Welland Canal get built, and other conveniences, while I live.

JOURNAL, March 17, 1842.

On Thoughts 🏵 🏵

🏵 My thoughts are my company.

JOURNAL, January 22, 1852.

🏵 Our thoughts are the epochs of our life: all else is but as a journal of the winds that blew while we were here.

JOURNAL, 1850.

🏵 All I can say is that I live and breathe and have my thoughts.

JOURNAL, 1850.

🏵 Each thought that is welcomed and recorded is a nest egg, by the side of which more will be laid.

JOURNAL, January 22, 1852.

🏵 Nothing was ever so unfamiliar and startling to me as my own thoughts.

JOURNAL, July 10, 1840.

🏵 The more you have thought and written on a given theme, the more you can still write. Thought breeds thought. It grows under your hands.

JOURNAL, February 13, 1860.

🏵 As the wild duck is more swift and beautiful than the tame, so is the wild—the mallard—thought, which 'mid falling dews wings its way above the fens.

WALKING.

🏵 The memorable thought, the happy expression, the admirable deed are only partly ours. The thought came to us because we were in a fit mood; also we were unconscious and did not know that we had said or done a good thing. We must walk consciously only part way toward our goal, and then leap in the dark to our success.

JOURNAL, March 11, 1859.

🏵 The fruit a thinker bears is *sentences*—statements or opinions. He seeks to affirm something as true. I am surprised that my affirmations or utterances come to me ready-made—not fore-thought—so that I occasionally awake in the night simply to let fall ripe a statement which I had never consciously considered before, and as surprising and novel and agreeable to me as anything can be.

JOURNAL, April 1, 186

🏵 There is no more Herculean task than to think thought about this life and then get it expressed.

JOURNAL, May 6,

❀ If I were confined to a corner of a garret all my days, like a spider, the world would be just as large to me while I had my thoughts about me.

WALDEN, Chapter XVIII.

❀ How can we expect a harvest of thought who have not had a seed-time of character?

JOURNAL, August 7, 1854.

❀ While I am abroad, the ovipositors plant their seeds in me; I am fly-blown with thought, and go home to hatch and brood over them.

JOURNAL, July 23, 1851.

❀ How rarely I meet a man who can be free, even in thought! We live according to rule. Some men are bed-ridden; all, world-ridden. I take my neighbor, an intellectual man, out into the woods and invite him to take a new and absolute view of things, to empty clean out of his thoughts all institutions of men and start again; but he can't do it, he sticks to his traditions and his crochets. He thinks that governments, colleges, newspapers, etc., are from everlasting to everlasting.

JOURNAL, May 12, 1857.

❀ The fathers and mothers of the town would rather hear the young man or young woman at their tables express reverence for some old statement of the truth than utter a direct revelation themselves. They don't want to have any prophets born into their families—damn them! So far as thinking is concerned, surely original thinking is the divinest thing. Rather we should reverently watch for the least motions, the least scintillations, of thought in this sluggish world, and men should run to and fro on the occasion more than at an earthquake.

JOURNAL, November 16, 1851.

❦ Our thoughts are wont to run in muddy or dusty ruts.

JOURNAL, 1850.

❦ My loftiest thought is somewhat like an eagle that suddenly comes into the field of view, suggesting great things and thrilling the beholder, as if it were bound hitherward with a message for me; but it comes no nearer, but circles and soars away, growing dimmer, disappointing me, till it is lost behind a cliff or a cloud.

JOURNAL, October 26, 1857.

❦ Time never passes so rapidly and unaccountably as when I am engaged in recording my thoughts. The world may perchance reach its end for us in a profounder thought, and Time itself run down.

JOURNAL, February 5, 1852.

❦ It is rare that we use our thinking faculty as resolutely as an Irishman his spade. To please our friends and relatives we turn out our silver ore in cartloads, while we neglect to work our mines of gold known only to ourselves far up in the Sierras, where we pulled up a bush in our mountain walk, and saw the glittering treasure. Let us return thither. Let it be the price of our freedom to make that known.

JOURNAL, January 13, 1852.

ON THOUGHTS

❧ Do not speak for other men; speak for yourself.

JOURNAL, December 25, 1851.

❧ I take it for granted, when I am invited to lecture anywhere—for I have had a little experience in that business—that there is a desire to hear what *I think* on some subject, though I may be the greatest fool in the country —and not that I should say pleasant things merely, or such as the audience will assent to; and I resolve, accordingly, that I will give them a strong dose of myself. They have sent for me, and engaged to pay for me, and I am determined that they shall have me, though I bore them beyond all precedent.

LIFE WITHOUT PRINCIPLE.

❧ Certainly it is a distinct profession to rescue from oblivion and to fix the sentiments and thoughts which visit all men more or less generally, that the contemplation of the unfinished picture may suggest its harmonious completion. Associate reverently and as much as you can with your loftiest thoughts.

JOURNAL, January 22, 1852.

❧ The thinker, he who is serene and self-possessed, is the brave, not the desperate soldier.

JOURNAL, May 6, 1858.

❧ Cars go by, and we know their substance as well as their shadow. They stop and we get into them. But those sublime thoughts passing on high do not stop, and we never get into them. Their conductor is not like one of us.

JOURNAL, 1851.

❦ Walking in the woods, it may be, some afternoon, the shadow of the wings of a thought flits across the landscape of my mind, and I am reminded how little eventful are our lives. What have been all these wars and rumors of wars, and modern discoveries and improvements so-called? A mere irritation of the skin. But this shadow which is so soon past, and whose substance is not detected, suggests that there are events of importance whose interval is to us a true historic period.

JOURNAL, 1851.

❦ Let me not be in haste to detect the *universal law;* let me see more clearly a particular instance of it!

JOURNAL, December 25, 1851.

❦ The greatest compliment that was ever paid me was when one asked me what *I thought,* and attended to my answer. I am surprised, as well as delighted, when this happens, it is such a rare use he would make of me, as if he were acquainted with the tool. Commonly, if men want anything of me, it is only to know how many acres I make of their land—since I am a surveyor—or, at most, what trivial news I have burdened myself with. They never will go to law for my meat; they prefer the shell.

LIFE WITHOUT PRINCIPLE.

❦ I saw a muskrat come out of a hole in the ice. While I am looking at him, I am thinking what he is thinking of me.

JOURNAL, November 25, 1850.

❦ Is not he hospitable who entertains thoughts?

JOURNAL, June 12, 1851.

ON THOUGHTS

※ The mere fragrance, rumor, and reminiscence of life is all that we get, for the most part. If I am visited by a thought, I chew that cud each successive morning, as long as there is any flavor in it. Until my keepers shake down some fresh fodder. Our genius is like a brush which only once in many months is freshly dipped into the paint-pot. It becomes so dry that though we apply it incessantly, it fails to tinge our earth and sky. Applied to the same spot incessantly, it at length imparts no color to it.

JOURNAL, August 9, 1858.

※ Has not the mind, too, its harvest? Do not some scarlet leaves of thought come scatteringly down, though it may be prematurely, some which, perchance, the summer's drought has ripened, and the rain loosed? Are there no purple reflections from the culms of thought in my mind?

JOURNAL, August 29, 1858.

※ Thoughts of different dates will not cohere.

JOURNAL, February 8, 1852.

※ Hold fast to your most indefinite, waking dream. The very green dust on the walls is an organized vegetable; the atmosphere has its fauna and flora floating in it; and shall we think that dreams are but dust and ashes, are always disintegrated and crumbling thoughts, and not dust-like thoughts trooping to their standard with music —systems beginning to be organized?

LETTER TO HARRISON BLAKE, February 27, 1853.

❀ How often the Saxon man talks of carrying out the designs of Providence, as if he had some knowledge of Providence and His designs. Men allow themselves to associate Providence and designs of Providence with their dull, prosaic, everyday thoughts of things.

JOURNAL, May 24, 1851.

❀ You *fail* in your thoughts, or you *prevail* in your thoughts only.

LETTER TO HARRISON BLAKE, September 26, 1859.

❀ When I was young and compelled to pass my Sunday in the house without the aid of interesting books, I used to spend many an hour till the wished-for sundown, watching the martins soar, from an attic window; and fortunate indeed did I deem myself when a hawk appeared in the heavens, though far toward the horizon against a downy cloud, and I searched for hours till I had found his mate. They, at least, took my thoughts from earthly things.

JOURNAL, April 17, 1852.

❀ The landscape lies far and fair within, and the deepest thinker is the farthest traveled.

A WALK TO WACHUSETT.

❀ When I could sit in a cold chamber muffled in a coat each evening till Thanksgiving time, warmed by my own thoughts, the world was not so much with me.

JOURNAL, September 27, 1852.

❀ Like cuttlefish we conceal ourselves, we darken the atmosphere in which we move; we are not transparent. I pine for one to whom I can speak my *first thoughts;* thoughts which represent me truly, which are no better and no worse than I; thoughts which have the bloom on them, which alone can be sacred and divine.

JOURNAL, August 24, 1852.

❀ What philosopher can estimate the different values of a waking thought and a dream?

JOURNAL, March 31, 1852.

❀ So there is one *thought* for the field, another for the house. I would have my thoughts, like wild apples, to be food for walkers, and will not warrant them to be palatable if tasted in the house.

WILD APPLES.

❀ You must walk like a camel, which is said to be the only beast which ruminates when it walks.

JOURNAL, 1850.

❀ Great thoughts hallow any labor. Today I earned seventy-five cents heaving manure out of a pen, and made a good bargain of it. If the ditcher muses the while how he may live uprightly, the ditching spade and turf knife may be engraved on the coat-of-arms of his posterity.

JOURNAL, April 20, 1841.

❀ You conquer fate by thought.

JOURNAL, May 6, 1858.

❀ As I stand over the insect crawling amid the pine needles on the forest floor, and endeavoring to conceal itself from my sight, and ask myself why it will cherish those humble thoughts, and hide its head from me who might, perhaps, be its benefactor, and impart to its race some cheering information, I am reminded of the greater Benefactor and Intelligence that stands over me the human insect.

WALDEN, Chapter XVIII.

❋ My thoughts have left no track, and I cannot find the path again.

WALDEN, Chapter XII.

❋ The at present unutterable things we may find somewhere uttered. These same questions that disturb and puzzle and confound us have in their turn occurred to all the wise men; not one has been omitted; and each has answered them, according to his ability, by his words and his life.

WALDEN, Chapter III.

❋ I delight to come to my bearings—not walk in procession with pomp and parade, in a conspicuous place, but to walk even with the Builder of the universe, if I may—not to live in this restless, nervous, bustling, trivial Nineteenth Century, but stand or sit thoughtfully while it goes by.

WALDEN, Chapter XVIII.

❋ He is a rich man, and enjoys the fruits of his riches, who summer and winter forever can find delight in his own thoughts.

THE WEEK, Friday.

On Simplicity 🦋 🦋

🦋 As for the complex ways of living, I love them not, however much I practice them. In as many places as possible, I will get my feet down to the earth.

JOURNAL, October 22, 1853.

🦋 Our life is frittered away by detail. An honest man has hardly need to count more than his ten fingers, or in extreme cases he may add his ten toes, and lump the rest. Simplicity, simplicity, simplicity! I say, let your affairs be as two or three, and not a hundred or a thousand; instead of a million count half a dozen, and keep your accounts on your thumbnail.

WALDEN, Chapter II.

🦋 Do not trouble yourself much to get new things, whether clothes or friends. Turn the old; return to them. Things do not change; we change.

WALDEN, Chapter XVIII.

It is astonishing as well as sad, how many trivial affairs even the wisest man thinks he must attend to in a day; how singular an affair he thinks he must omit. When the mathematician would solve a difficult problem, he first frees the equation of all incumbrances, and reduces it to its simplest terms. So simplify the problem of life, distinguish the necessary and the real. Probe the earth and see where your main roots run.

LETTER TO HARRISON BLAKE, March 27, 1848.

The savage lives simply through ignorance and idleness or laziness, but the philosopher lives simply through wisdom.

JOURNAL, September 1, 1853.

A party of school-children had a picnic at the Esterbrooks Country the other day, and they carried bags of beans from their gymnasium to exercise with there. I cannot be interested in these extremely artificial amusements. The traveller is no longer a wayfarer, with his staff and pack and dusty coat. He is not a pilgrim, but he travels in a saloon, and carries dumb-bells to exercise with in the intervals of his journey.

JOURNAL, October 10, 1860.

Again and again I am surprised to observe what an interval there is, in what is called civilized life, between the shell and the inhabitant of the shell—what a disproportion there is between the life of man and his conveniences and luxuries.

JOURNAL, September 16, 1859.

It is glorious to consider how independent man is of all enervating luxuries; and the poorer he is in respect to them, the richer he is.

JOURNAL, November 22, 1860.

We are often reminded that if there were bestowed on us the wealth of Croesus, our aims must still be the same, and our means essentially the same. Moreover, if you are restricted in your range by poverty, if you cannot buy books and newspapers, for instance, you are but confined to the most significant and vital experiences; you are compelled to deal with the material which yields the most sugar and the most starch. It is life near the bone where it is sweetest. You are defended from being a trifler. No man loses ever on a lower plane by magnanimity on a higher.

WALDEN, Chapter XVIII.

There are two kinds of simplicity—one that is akin to foolishness, the other to wisdom. The philosopher's style of living is only outwardly simple, but inwardly complex. The savage's style is both outwardly and inwardly simple. A simpleton can perform many mechanical labors, but is not capable of profound thought. It was their limited view, not in respect to *style*, but to the *object* of living. A man who has equally limited views with respect to the end of living will not be helped by the most complex and refined style of living. It is not the tub that makes Diogenes, the Jove-born, but Diogenes the tub.

JOURNAL, September 1, 1853.

The too exquisitely cultured I avoid as I do the theater. Their life lacks reality. They offer me wine instead of water. They are surrounded by things that can be bought.

JOURNAL, June 26, 1852.

It is well to find your employment and amusement in simple and homely things. These wear best and yield most. I think I would rather watch the motions of these cows in their pasture for a day, which I now see all headed one way and slowly advancing—watch them and project their course carefully on a chart, and report all their behavior faithfully—than wander to Europe or Asia and watch other motions there; for it is only ourselves that we report in either case, and perchance we shall report a more restless and worthless self in the latter case than in the first.

JOURNAL, October 5, 1856.

We have heard a great deal about English comfort. But may you not trace these stories home to some wealthy Sardanapalus who was able to pay for obsequious attendance and for every luxury? Ask the great mass of Englishmen and travellers, whose vote alone is conclusive, concerning the comfort they enjoyed in second and third class accommodations in steamboats and railroads and eating and lodging houses. Lord Somebody-or-other may have made himself comfortable, but the very style of his living makes it necessary that the great majority of his countrymen should be uncomfortable.

JOURNAL, January 14, 1852.

ON SIMPLICITY

🐝 A lady once offered me a mat, but as I had no room to spare within the house, nor time to spare within or without to shake it, I declined it, preferring to wipe my feet on the sod before my door. It is best to avoid the beginnings of evil.

WALDEN, Chapter I.

🐝 At the present day, and in this country, as I find by my own experience, a few implements, a knife, an axe, a spade, a wheelbarrow, etc., and for the studious, lamplight, stationery, and access to a few books, rank next to necessities, and can all be obtained at a trifling cost. Yet some, not wise, go to the other side of the globe, to barbarous and unhealthy regions, and devote themselves to trade for ten or twenty years, in order that they may live—that is, keep comfortably warm—and die in New England at last.

WALDEN, Chapter I.

🐝 To what end do I lead a simple life at all, pray? That I may teach others to simplify their lives?—and so all our lives be *simplified* merely, like an algebraic formula? Or not, rather, that I may make use of the ground I have cleared to live more worthily and profitably?

LETTER TO HARRISON BLAKE, September 26, 1855.

On Nature ❇ ❇

❇ I have a room all to myself; it is nature.

JOURNAL, *January 3, 1853.*

❇ There are two worlds, the post-office and nature. I know them both.

JOURNAL, *January 3, 1853.*

❇ Ah, dear nature, the mere remembrance, after a short forgetfulness, of the pine woods! I come to it as a hungry man to a crust of bread.

JOURNAL, *December 12, 1851.*

❇ Olympus is the outside of the earth everywhere.

JOURNAL, *May 30, 1853.*

❇ Nature would not appear so rich, the profusion so rich, if we knew a use for everything.

JOURNAL, *August 11, 1853.*

❦ Man and his affairs, church and state and school, trade and commerce, and manufactures and agriculture, even politics, the most alarming of them all—I am pleased to see how little space they occupy in the landscape.

WALKING.

❦ In the forenoon commonly I see nature only through a window; in the afternoon my study or apartment in which I sit is a vale.

JOURNAL, October 8, 1851.

❦ Sophia says, bringing company into my sanctum, by way of apology, that I regard the dust on my furniture like the bloom on fruits, not to be swept off. Which reminds me that the bloom on fruits and stems is the only dust which settles on Nature's furniture.

JOURNAL, September 15, 1856.

❦ One might say that the yellow of the earth mingled with the blue of the sky to make the green of vegetation.

JOURNAL, March 8, 1859.

❦ I love Nature partly *because* she is not man, but a retreat from him. None of his institutions control or pervade her. There a different kind of right prevails. In her midst I can be glad with an entire gladness. If this world were all man, I could not stretch myself, I should lose all hope. He is constraint, she is freedom to me. He makes me wish for another world. She makes me content with this.

JOURNAL, January 3, 1853.

✻ It appears to be a law that you cannot have a deep sympathy with both man and nature. Those qualities which bring you near to the one estrange you from the other.

JOURNAL, April 11, 1852.

✻ There can be no very black melancholy to him who lives in the midst of nature and has his senses still.

WALDEN, Chapter V.

✻ Nature and man; some prefer the one, others the other; but that is all *de gustibus*. It makes no odds at what well you drink, provided it be a well-head.

JOURNAL, 1851.

✻ There are odors enough in nature to remind you of everything, if you had lost every sense but smell.

JOURNAL, May 6, 1852.

✻ I am refreshed and expanded when the freight train rattles past me, and I smell the stores which go dispensing their odors all the way from Long Wharf to Lake Champlain, reminding me of foreign parts, of coral reefs, and Indian oceans, and tropical climes, and the extent of the globe.

WALDEN, Chapter IV.

✻ What has become of Nature's common sense and love of facts, when in the very mud-puddles she reflects the skies and trees?

JOURNAL, November 9, 1851.

How nicely Nature is adjusted! The motion of a particle of dust on the surface of any brook far inland shows which way the earth declines toward the sea, which way lies the constantly descending route, and the only one.

JOURNAL, December 22, 1859.

We, too, are out, obeying the same law with all nature. Not less important are the observers of the birds than the birds themselves.

JOURNAL, March 20, 1858.

When I find a new and rare plant in Concord I seem to think it has but just sprung up here—that it is, and not I am, the newcomer—while it has grown here for ages before I was born.

JOURNAL, September 2, 1856.

If any part of nature excites our pity, it is for ourselves we grieve, for there is eternal health and beauty. We get only transient and partial glimpses of the beauty of the world. Standing at the right angle, we are dazzled by the colors of the rainbow in colorless ice. From the right point of view, every storm and every drop in it is a rainbow. Beauty and music are not mere traits and exceptions. They are the rule and character. It is the exception that we see and hear.

JOURNAL, December 11, 1855.

How many of our troubles are house-bred!

JOURNAL, March 28, 1858.

I wonder that houses are not oftener located mainly that they may command particular rare prospects, every convenience yielding to this. The farmer would never suspect what it was you were buying, and such sites would be the cheapest of any.

JOURNAL, May 25, 1851.

The true sites for human dwellings are unimproved.

JOURNAL, May 25, 1851.

Some of our richest days are those in which no sun shines outwardly, but so much the more a sun shines inwardly. I love nature, I love the landscape, because it is so sincere. It never cheats me. It never jests. It is cheerfully, musically earnest.

JOURNAL, November 16, 1850.

I do not know where to find in any literature, whether ancient or modern, any adequate account of that Nature with which I am acquainted. Mythology comes nearest to it of any.

JOURNAL, February, 1851.

What is a chamber to which the sun does not rise in the morning? What is a chamber to which the sun does not set at evening? Such are often the chambers of the mind, for the most part.

JOURNAL, April 30, 1851.

We are wont to forget that the sun looks on our cultivated fields and on the prairies and forests without distinction. They all reflect and absorb his rays alike, and the former make but a small part of the glorious picture which he beholds in his daily course. In his view the earth is all equally cultivated like a garden.

WALDEN, *Chapter VII.*

⚜ Nature will bear the closest inspection; she invites us to lay our eye level with the smallest leaf, and take an insect view of its plain. She has no interstices; every part is full of life.

NATURAL HISTORY OF MASSACHUSETTS.

⚜ Why do precisely these objects which we behold make a world? Why has man just these species of animals for his neighbors; as if nothing but a mouse could have filled this crevice?

WALDEN, *Chapter XII.*

⚜ The perch swallows the grub-worm, the pickerel swallows the perch, and the fisherman swallows the pickerel; and so all the chinks in the scale of being are filled.

WALDEN, *Chapter XVI.*

⚜ I love to see that Nature is so rife with life that myriads can be afforded to be sacrificed and suffered to prey on one another; that tender organizations can be so serenely squashed out of existence like pulp—tadpoles which herons gobble up, and tortoises and toads run over in the road; and that sometimes it has rained flesh and blood! With the liability to accident, we must see how little account is to be made of it.

WALDEN, *Chapter XVII.*

⚜ Nature invites fire to sweep her floors, for purification.

JOURNAL, *May 5, 1852.*

�֎ The constitution of the Indian mind appears to be the very opposite of that of the white man. He is acquainted with a different side of nature. He measures his life by winters, not summers. His year is not measured by the sun, but consists of a certain number of moons, and his moons are not measured by days, but by nights. He has taken hold of the dark side of nature; the white man, the bright side.

JOURNAL, October 25, 1852.

✿ There is no law so strong which a little gladness may not transgress. Pile up your books, the records of sadness, your saws and your laws. Nature is glad outside, and her merry worms within will ere long topple them down.

JOURNAL, January 3, 1853.

✿ The Maker of this earth but patented a leaf.

WALDEN, Chapter XVII.

✿ The man of science, who is not seeking for expression but for a fact to be expressed merely, studies nature as a dead language. I pray for such inward experience as will make nature significant.

JOURNAL, May 10, 1853.

✿ How happens it we reverence the stones which fall from another planet, and not the stones which belong to this—another globe, not this—heaven, and not earth? Are not the stones in Hodge's wall as good as the aerolite at Mecca? Is not our broad back-door-stone as good as any corner-stone in heaven?

JOURNAL, August 30, 1856.

After having some business dealings with men, I am occasionally chagrined, and feel as if I had done some wrong, and it is hard to forget the ugly circumstance. I see that such intercourse long continued would make one thoroughly prosaic, hard, and course. But the longest intercourse with Nature, though in her rudest moods, does not thus harden and make coarse. A hard, insensible man whom we liken to a rock is indeed much harder than a rock. From hard, coarse, insensible men with whom I have no sympathy, I go to commune with the rocks, whose hearts are comparatively soft.

JOURNAL, November 15, 1853.

How important is a constant intercourse with nature and the contemplation of natural phenomena to the preservation of moral and intellectual health! The discipline of the schools or of business can never impart such serenity to the mind.

JOURNAL, May 6, 1851.

We are interested in the phenomena of Nature mainly as children are, or as we are in games of chance. They are more or less exciting. Our appetite for novelty is insatiable. We do not attend to ordinary things, though they are most important, but to extraordinary ones.

JOURNAL, March 19, 1859.

When we can no longer ramble in the fields of nature, we ramble in the fields of thought and literature. The old become readers. Our heads retain their strength when our legs have become weak.

JOURNAL, 1851.

✻ Books of natural history make the most cheerful winter reading. I read in Audubon with a thrill of delight, when the snow covers the ground, of the magnolia, and the Florida keys, and their warm sea breezes: of the fence-rail and the cotton-tree, and the migration of the rice-bird; or of the breaking up of winter in Labrador. I seem to hear the melting of the snow on the forks of the Missouri as I read. I imbibe some portion of health from these reminiscenses of luxuriant nature.

JOURNAL, December 31, 1841.

✻ I should like to keep some book of natural history always by me as a sort of elixir, the reading of which would restore the tone of my system and secure me true and cheerful views of life.

JOURNAL, December 31, 1841.

✻ With man all is uncertainty. He does not confidently look forward to another spring. But examine the root of the savory-leaved aster, and you will find the new shoots, fair purple shoots, which are to curve upward and bear the next year's flowers, already grown half an inch or more in earth. Nature is confident.

JOURNAL, October 12, 1858.

✻ Nature has left nothing to the mercy of man.

JOURNAL, March 22, 1861.

On Books ⚜ ⚜

⚜ Read the best books first, or you may not have a chance to read them at all.

THE WEEK, Sunday.

⚜ He who cannot read is worse than deaf and blind, is yet but half alive, is still-born.

JOURNAL, March 10, 1856.

⚜ A book should contain pure discoveries, glimpses of *terra firma*, though by shipwrecked mariners, and not the art of navigation by those who have never been out of sight of land.

THE WEEK, Sunday.

⚜ How many a man has dated a new era in his life from the reading of a book!

WALDEN, Chapter III.

For the most part an author but consults with all who have written before upon any subject, and his book is but the advice of so many. But a true book will never have been forestalled, but the topic itself will be new, and, by consulting with nature, it will consult not only with those who have gone before, but with those who may come after. There is always room and occasion enough for a true book on any subject, as there is room for more light the brightest day, and more rays will not interfere with the first.

JOURNAL, *March 13, 1841.*

In a true history or biography, of how little consequence those events of which so much is commonly made! For example, how difficult for a man to remember in what towns or houses he has lived, or when! Yet one of the first steps of his biographer will be to establish these facts, and he will thus give an undue importance to many of them. I find in my Journal that the most important events in my life, if recorded at all, are not dated.

JOURNAL, *December 26, 1855.*

All that are printed and bound are not books; they do not necessarily belong to letters, but are oftener to be ranked with the other luxuries and appendages of civilized life. Base wares are palmed off under a thousand disguises.

THE WEEK, *Sunday.*

Scholars have for the most part a diseased way of looking at the world. They mean by it a few cities and unfortunate assemblies of men and women, who might all be concealed in the grass of the prairies. They describe the world as old or new, healthy or diseased, according to the state of their libraries—a little dust more or less on their shelves.

JOURNAL, 1837–47.

⚹ Most books belong to the house and street only, and in the fields their leaves feel very thin. They are bare and obvious, and have no halo or haze about them. Nature lies far and fair behind them all.

THE WEEK, Monday.

⚹ It is the untamed, uncivilized, free, and wild thinking in Hamlet, in the Illiad, and in all the scriptures and mythologies that delights us—not learned in the schools, not refined and polished by art. A truly good book is something as wildly natural and primitive, mysterious and marvelous, ambrosial and fertile, as a fungus or a lichen. Suppose the muskrat or beaver were to turn his views to literature, what fresh views of nature would he present!

JOURNAL, November 16, 1850.

⚹ Most events recorded in history are more remarkable than important, like eclipses of the sun and moon, by which all are attracted, but whose effect no one takes the trouble to calculate.

THE WEEK, Monday.

⚹ By dint of able writing and pen-craft, books are cunningly compiled, and have their run and success even among the learned, as if they were the result of a new man's thinking, and their birth is attended with some natural throes. But in a little while their covers fall off, for no binding will avail, and it appears that they are not Books or Bibles at all. There are new and patented inventions in this shape, purporting to be for the elevation of the race, which many a pure scholar and genius who has learned to read is for a moment deceived by, and finds himself reading a horse-rake, or spinning-jenny, or wooden nutmeg, or oak-leaf cigar, or steam-power press, or kitchen range, perchance, when he was seeking serene and biblical truths.

THE WEEK, *Sunday.*

After all, I believe it is the style of thought entirely, and not the style of expression, which makes the difference in books.

JOURNAL, March 23, 1842.

Books are for the most part willfully and hastily written, as parts of a system to supply a want real or imagined. Books of natural history aim commonly to be hasty schedules, or inventories of God's property, by some clerk. They do not in the least teach the divine view of nature, but the popular view, or rather the popular method of studying nature, and make haste to conduct the persevering pupil only into that dilemma where the profesors always dwell.

THE WEEK, *Sunday.*

Wherever men have lived there is a story to be told, and it depends chiefly on the story-teller or historian whether it is interesting or not.

JOURNAL, March 18, 1861.

44

So far as the natural history is concerned, you often have your choice between uninteresting truth and interesting falsehood.

JOURNAL, March 5, 1860.

A truly good book attracts very little favor to itself. It is so true that it teaches me better than to read it. I must soon lay it down and commence living on its hint.

JOURNAL, February 19, 1841.

When I read an indifferent book, it seems the best thing I can do, but the inspiring volume hardly leaves me leisure to finish its latter pages. It is slipping out of my fingers while I read. It creates no atmosphere in which it may be perused, but one in which its teachings may be practiced. It confers on me such wealth that I lay it down with the least regret. What I began by reading I must finish by acting.

JOURNAL, February 19, 1841.

The Library is a wilderness of books. Looking over books on Canada written within the last three hundred years, could see how one had been built upon another, each author consulting and referring to his predecessors. You could read most of them without changing your legs on the steps. It is necessary to find out exactly what books to read on a given subject. Though there may be a thousand books written upon it, it is only important to read three or four; they will contain all that is essential, and a few pages will show which they are. Books which are books are all that you want, and there are but half a dozen in any thousand.

JOURNAL, March 16, 1852.

✻ Many college text-books which were a weariness and a stumbling-block when *studied*, I have since read a little in with pleasure and profit.

JOURNAL, February 19, 1854.

✻ Certainly, we do not need to be soothed and entertained always like children. He who resorts to the easy novel, because he is languid, does no better than if he took a nap. The front aspect of great thoughts can only be enjoyed by those who stand on the side whence they arrive. Books, not which afford us a cowering enjoyment, but in which each thought is of unusual daring; such as an idle man cannot read, and a timid one would not be entertained by, which even make us dangerous to existing institutions—such call I good books.

THE WEEK, Sunday.

✻ If men were to be destroyed and the books they have written were to be transmitted to a new race of creatures, in a new world, what kind of record would be found in them of so remarkable a phenomenon as the rainbow?

JOURNAL, March 13, 1859.

✻ The woodchopper reads the wisdom of the ages recorded on the paper that holds his dinner, then lights his pipe with it. When we ask for a scrap of paper for the most trivial use, it may have the confessions of Augustine or the sonnets of Shakespeare, and we not observe it. The student kindles his fire, the editor packs his trunk, the sportsman loads his gun, the traveler wraps his dinner, the Irishman papers his shanty, the schoolboy peppers the plastering, the belle pins up her hair, with the printed thoughts of men.

JOURNAL, March 10, 1856.

On Freedom ❋ ❋

❋ It is hard to have a Southern overseer; it is worse to have a Northern one; but worst of all when you are yourself the slave-driver.

JOURNAL, 1845–47.

❋ Do we call this the land of the free? What is it to be free from King George the Fourth and continue the slaves of prejudice? What is it to be born free and equal, and not to live? What is the value of any political freedom, but as a means to moral freedom?

JOURNAL, February 16, 1851.

❋ Men talk of freedom! How many are free to think? Free from fear, from perturbation, from prejudice? Nine hundred and ninety-nine in a thousand are perfect slaves.

JOURNAL, May 6, 1858.

✳ The mass of men are very easily imposed on. They have their runways in which they always travel, and are sure to fall into any pit or box-trap set therein.

JOURNAL, November 28, 1860.

✳ What we want is not mainly to colonize Nebraska with free men, but to colonize Massachusetts with free men—to be free ourselves. As the enterprise of a few individuals, that is brave and practical; but as the enterprise of the State, it is cowardice and imbecility. What odds where we squat, or how much ground we cover? It is not the soil that we would make free, but men.

JOURNAL, June 18, 1854.

✳ What great interval is there between him who is caught in Africa and made a plantation slave of in the South, and him who is caught in New England and made a Unitarian minister of?

JOURNAL, February 28, 1857.

✳ Talk about slavery! It is not the peculiar institution of the South. It exists wherever men are bought and sold, wherever a man allows himself to be made a mere thing or a tool, and surrenders his inalienable rights of reason and conscience. Indeed this slavery is more complete than that which enslaves the body alone. It exists in the Northern States, and I am reminded by what I find in the newspapers that it exists in Canada. I never yet met with, or heard of, a judge who was not a slave of this kind, and so the finest and most unfailing weapon of injustice. He fetches a slightly higher price than the black man only because he is a more valuable slave.

JOURNAL, December 4, 1860.

ON FREEDOM

✳ The question is whether you can bear freedom. At present the vast majority of men, whether white or black, require the discipline of labor which enslaves them for their own good.

JOURNAL, September 1, 1853.

✳ Why should we be in such desperate haste to succeed and in such desperate enterprises? If a man does not keep pace with his companions, perhaps it is because he hears a different drummer. Let him step to the music which he hears, however measured or far away.

WALDEN, Chapter XVIII.

✳ We have used up all our inherited freedom, like the young bird the albumen in the egg. It is not an era of repose. If we would save our lives, we must fight for them.

JOURNAL, June 16, 1854.

On the Uses of Time ✍ ✍

✍ Time is the stream I go a-fishing in. I drink at it; but while I drink I see the sandy bottom and detect how shallow it is. Its thin current slides away, but eternity remains. I would drink deeper; fish in the sky, whose bottom is pebbly with stars.

WALDEN, Chapter II.

✍ I wish to suggest that a man may be very industrious, and yet not spend his time well. There is no more fatal blunderer than he who consumes the greater part of life getting his living.

LIFE WITHOUT PRINCIPLE.

✍ As boys are sometimes required to show an excuse for being absent from school, so it seems to me that men should have to show some excuse for being here.

JOURNAL, January 3, 1861.

ON THE USES OF TIME

↗ Nothing can be more useful to a man than a determination not to be hurried.

JOURNAL, March 22, 1842.

↗ I had three pieces of limestone on my desk, but I was terrified to find that they required to be dusted daily, when the furniture of my mind was all undusted still, and I threw them out the window in disgust.

WALDEN, Chapter I.

↗ June, July, and August, the tortoise eggs are hatching a few inches beneath the surface in sandy fields. You tell of active labors, of works of art, and wars the past summer; meanwhile the tortoise eggs underlie this turmoil. What events have transpired on the lit and airy surface three inches above them! Summer knocked down; Kansas living an age of suspense. Think what is a summer to them! How many worthy men have died and had their funeral sermons preached since I saw the mother turtle bury her eggs here! They contained an undeveloped liquid then, they are now turtles. June, July, and August —the livelong summer—what are they with their heats and fevers but sufficient to hatch a tortoise in. Be not in haste; mind your private affairs. Consider the turtle. A whole summer—June, July, and August—is not too good nor too much to hatch a turtle in. Perchance you have worried yourself, despaired of the world, meditated the end of life, and all things seemed rushing to destruction; but nature has steadily and serenely advanced with a turtle's pace.

JOURNAL, August 28, 1856.

✍ My purpose in going to Walden Pond was not to live cheaply nor to live dearly there, but to transact some private business with the fewest obstacles; to be hindered from accomplishing which for want of a little common sense, a little enterprise and business talent, appeared not so sad as foolish.

WALDEN, Chapter I.

✍ Do what nobody can do for you. Omit to do everything else.

JOURNAL, 1850.

✍ Keep the time, observe the hours of the universe, not of the cars.

JOURNAL, December 28, 1852.

✍ I know many men who, in common things, are not to be deceived; who trust no moonshine; who count their money correctly, and know how to invest it; who are said to be prudent and knowing, who yet will stand at a desk the greater part of their lives, as cashiers in banks, and glimmer and rust and finally go out there. If they *know* anything, what under the sun do they do that for? Do they know what *bread* is? or what it is for? Do they know what life is? If they *knew* something, the places which know them now would know them no more forever.

LETTER TO HARRISON BLAKE, March 27, 1848.

✍ He that is not behind his time is swift.

JOURNAL, September 13, 1852.

ON THE USES OF TIME

🖋 We are inclined to think of all Romans who lived within five hundred years B.C. as *contemporaries* to each other. Yet Time moved at the same deliberate pace then as now.

JOURNAL, December 8, 1859.

🖋 How earnestly and rapidly each creature, each flower, is fulfilling its part while its day lasts! Nature never lost a day nor a moment. As the planet in its orbit and around its axis, so do the seasons, so does time, revolve, with a rapidity inconceivable. In the moment, in the aeon, well employed, time ever advances with this rapidity.

JOURNAL, September 13, 1852.

🖋 If I shall sell both my forenoons and afternoons to society, as most appear to do, I am sure that for me there would be nothing left worth living for. I trust that I shall never thus sell my birthright for a mess of pottage.

LIFE WITHOUT PRINCIPLE.

🖋 There is a coarse and boisterous money-making fellow in the outskirts of our town who is going to build a blank-wall under the hill along the edge of his meadow. The powers have put this into his head to keep him out of mischief, and he wishes me to spend three weeks digging there with him. The result will be that he will perhaps get some more money to hoard, and leave for his heirs to spend foolishly. If I do this, most will commend me as an industrious and hard-working man; but if I choose to devote myself to certain labors which yield more real profit, though but little money, they may be inclined to look on me as an idler. Nevertheless, as I do not need the police of meaningless labor to regulate me, and do not see anything absolutely praiseworthy in this fellow's undertaking any more than in many an enterprise of our own or foreign governments, however amusing it may be to him or them, I prefer to finish my education at a different school.

LIFE WITHOUT PRINCIPLE.

I *live* in the *present*. I only remember the past, and anticipate the future.

LETTER TO HARRISON BLAKE, March 27, 1848.

Both for bodily and mental health, court the present.

JOURNAL, December 28, 1852.

Time hides no treasures; we want not its *then*, but its *now*.

JOURNAL, August 9, 1841.

It is reasonable that a man should be something worthier at the end of the year than he was at the beginning.

JOURNAL, March 15, 1852.

What's the use of ushering the day with prayer, if it is thus consecrated to turning a few more pennies merely? All genuine goodness is original and as free from cant and tradition as the air.

JOURNAL, June 16, 1857.

✍ Time is cheap and rather insignificant. It matters not whether it is a river which changes from side to side in a geological period or an eel that wriggles past in an instant.

JOURNAL, March 24, 1855.

✍ I am invited to take some party of ladies or gentlemen on an excursion—to walk or sail, or the like—but by all kinds of evasions I omit it, and am thought to be rude and unaccommodating therefore. They do not consider that the wood-path and the boat are my studio, where I maintain a sacred solitude and cannot admit promiscuous company. I will see them occasionally in the evening or at the table, however. They do not think of taking a child away from its school to go a-huckleberrying with them. Why should not I, then, have my school and school hours to be respected? Ask me for a certain number of dollars if you will, but do not ask me for my afternoons.

JOURNAL, September 16, 1859.

✍ Go not so far out of your way for a truer life; keep strictly onward in that path alone which your genius points out. Do the things which lie nearest to you, but which are difficult to do.

JOURNAL, January 12, 1852.

✍ Each man's necessary path, though as obscure and apparently uneventful as that of a beetle in the grass, is the way to the deepest joys he is susceptible of; though he converses only with moles and fungi and disgraces his relatives, it is no matter if he knows what is steel to his flint.

JOURNAL, November 18, 1857.

55

✍ The fruitless enterprise of some persons who rush helter-skelter, carrying out their crazy scheme—merely "putting it through" as they phrase it—reminds me of those thistle-downs which, not being detained nor steadied by any seed at the base, are blown away at the first impulse and go rolling over all obstacles. They may indeed go fastest and farthest, but where they rest at last not even a thistle springs.

JOURNAL, November 17, 1858.

✍ If you can drive a nail and have any nails to drive, drive them.

JOURNAL, 1850.

✍ The longer the lever, the less perceptible its motion. It is the slowest pulsation which is most vital. The hero then will know how to wait, as well as to make haste. All good abides with him who waiteth *wisely;* we shall sooner overtake the dawn by remaining here than by hurrying over the hills of the west.

THE WEEK, Monday.

✍ Pursue some path, however narrow and crooked, in which you can walk with love and reverence. Wherever a man separates from the multitude and goes his own way, there is a fork in the road, though the travelers along the highway see only a gap in the paling.

JOURNAL, October 18, 1855.

✍ When I see a stone which it must have taken many yoke of oxen to move, lying in a bank wall which was built two hundred years ago, I am curiously surprised, because it suggests an energy and force of which we have no memorials. Where are the traces of the corresponding moral and intellectual energy?

JOURNAL, 1850.

This spending of the best part of one's life earning money in order to enjoy a questionable liberty during the least valuable part of it reminds me of the Englishman who went to India to make a fortune first, in order that he might return to England and live the life of a poet. He should have gone up garret at once.

WALDEN, Chapter I.

I do not remember any page which will tell me how to spend this afternoon. I do not so much wish to know how to economize time as how to spend it, by what means to grow rich, that the day may not have been in vain.

JOURNAL, September 7, 1851.

Do what you reprove yourself for not doing. Know that you are neither satisfied nor dissatisfied with yourself without reason.

JOURNAL, 1850.

Let me say to you and to myself in one breath: Cultivate the tree which you have found to bear fruit in your soil. Regard not your past failures nor successes. All the past is equally a failure and a success; it is a success in as much as it offers you the present opportunity.

JOURNAL, 1850.

57

✍ It is not worth the while to go round the world to count the cats in Zanzibar.

WALDEN, Chapter XVIII.

✍ What means this sense of lateness that so comes over one now—as if the rest of the year were downhill, and if we had not performed anything before, we should not now? The season of flowers or of promise may be said to be over, and now is the season of fruits; but where is our fruit? The night of the year is approaching. What have we done with our talent? All nature prompts and reproves us. How early in the year it begins to be late!

JOURNAL, August 18, 1853.

✍ We are shown fair scenes in order that we may be tempted to inhabit them, and not simply tell what we have seen.

JOURNAL, November 24, 1857.

✍ I just put another stick into my stove—a pretty large mass of white oak. How many men will do enough this cold winter to pay for the fuel that will be required to warm them? I suppose I have burned up a pretty good-sized tree tonight—and for what? I settled with Mr. Tarbell for it the other day; but that wasn't the final settlement. I got off cheaply from him. At last, one will say, "Let me see, how much wood did you burn, Sir?" And I shall shudder to think that the next question will be, "What did you do while you were warm?"

LETTER TO HARRISON BLAKE, December 19, 1854.

On Wildness 🌿 🌿

🌿 We need the tonic of wildness—to wade sometimes in marshes where the bittern and the meadow-hen lurk, and hear the booming of the snipe; to smell the whispering sedge where only some wilder and more solitary fowl builds her nest, and the mink crawls with its belly close to the ground.

WALDEN, Chapter XVII.

🌿 In Wildness is the preservation of the World.

WALKING.

🌿 I wish my neighbors were wilder.

JOURNAL, 1851.

🌿 Men come tamely home at night only from the next field or street, where their household echoes haunt, and their life pines because it breathes its own breath over again; their shadows, morning and evening, reach farther than their daily steps. We would come home from far, from adventures, and perils, and discoveries every day, with new experience and character.

WALDEN, Chapter X.

❧ I should be pleased to meet man in the woods. I wish he were to be encountered like wild caribous and moose.

JOURNAL, June 18, 1840.

❧ We would not always be soothing and taming nature, breaking the horse and the ox, but sometimes ride the horse wild and chase the buffalo.

THE WEEK, Sunday.

❧ The journals think they cannot say too much on improvements in husbandry. It is a safe theme, like piety. But for me, as for one of these farms brushed up—a model farm—I had as lief see a patent churn and a man turning it. It is simply a place where somebody is making money.

JOURNAL, February 27, 1858.

❧ I wish to speak a word for Nature, for absolute freedom and wildness, as contrasted with a freedom and culture merely civil—to regard man as an inhabitant, or a part and parcel of Nature, rather than a member of society.

WALKING.

❧ To see the larger and wilder birds, you must go forth in the great storms like this. At such times they frequent our neighborhood and trust themselves in our midst. A life of fair-weather walks *might* never show you the goose sailing on our waters, or the great heron feeding here. When the storm increases, then these great birds that carry the mail of the seasons lay to. To see wild life you must go forth at a wild season.

JOURNAL, April 19, 1852.

✿ Life consists with wildness. The most alive is the wildest.

WALKING.

✿ Let a slight snow come and cover the earth, and the tracks of men will show how little the woods and fields are frequented.

JOURNAL, February 3, 1857.

✿ What shall we do with a man who is afraid of the woods, their solitude and darkness? What salvation is there for him? God is silent and mysterious.

JOURNAL, November 16, 1850.

✿ Every landscape which is dreary enough has a certain beauty to my eyes.

CAPE COD, Chapter III.

✿ There are some intervals which border the strain of the wood thrush, to which I would migrate—wild lands where no settler has squatted; to which, methinks, I am already acclimated.

WALKING.

✿ When, formerly, I have analyzed my partiality for some farm which I had contemplated purchasing, I have

61

frequently found that I was attracted solely by a few square rods of impermeable and unfathomable bog—a natural sink in one corner of it. That was the jewel which dazzled me. I derive more of my subsistence from the swamps which surround my native town than from the cultivated gardens in the village.

WALKING.

In literature it is only the wild that attracts us. Dullness is but another name for tameness.

WALKING.

It is in vain to dream of a wildness distant from ourselves. There is none such. It is the bog in our brain and bowels, the primitive vigor of Nature in us, that inspires that dream. I shall never find in the wilds of Labrador any greater wildness than in some recess in Concord, i.e. than I import into it.

JOURNAL, August 30, 1856.

Ah, bless the Lord, O my soul! Bless him for wildness, for crows that will not alight within gunshot! and bless him for hens, too, that croak and cackle in the yard!

JOURNAL, January 12, 1855.

I long for wildness, a nature which I cannot put my foot through, woods where the wood thrush forever sings, where the hours are early morning ones, and there is dew on the grass, and the day is forever unproved, where I might have a fertile unknown for a soil about me. I would go after the cows, I would watch the flocks of Admetus there forever, only for my board and clothes.

JOURNAL, June 22, 1853.

❧ As I came home through the woods with my string of fish, trailing my pole, it being now quite dark, I caught a glimpse of a woodchuck stealing across my path, and felt a strange thrill of savage delight, and was strongly tempted to seize and devour him raw; not that I was hungry then, except for that wildness which he represented.

WALDEN, *Chapter XI.*

❧ At the same time that we are earnest to explore and learn all things, we require that all things be mysterious and unexplorable, that land and sea be infinitely wild, unsurveyed and unfathomed by us because unfathomable. We can never have enough of nature. We must be refreshed by the sight of inexhaustible vigor, vast and titanic features, the sea-coast with its wrecks, the wilderness with its living and its decaying trees, the thunder-cloud, and the rain which lasts three weeks and produces freshets. We need to witness our own limits transgressed, and some life pasturing freely where we never wander.

WALDEN, *Chapter XVII.*

❧ The universe is larger than enough for man's abode. Some rarely go outdoors, most are always at home at night, very few indeed have stayed out all night once in their lives, fewer still have gone behind the world of humanity, seen its institutions like toadstools by the wayside.

JOURNAL, *April 2, 1852.*

❧ What we call wildness is a civilization other than our own.

JOURNAL, *February 16, 1859.*

63

I enter some glade in the woods, perchance, where a few weeds and dry leaves alone lift themselves above the surface of snow, and it is as if I had come to an open window. I see out and around myself. Our *skylights* are thus far away from the ordinary resorts of men. I am not satisfied with ordinary windows. I must have a true *skylight*.

JOURNAL, January 7, 1857.

Nowadays almost all man's improvements, so called, as the building of houses and the cutting down of the forest and of all large trees, simply deform the landscape, and make it more and more tame and cheap.

WALKING.

When a farmer cleans out his ditches, I mourn the loss of many a flower which he calls a weed.

JOURNAL, April 10, 1853.

Whatever has not come under the sway of man is wild. In this sense original and independent men are wild —not tamed and broken by society.

JOURNAL, September 3, 1851.

On Wealth 🖋 🖋

🖋 A man is rich in proportion to the number of things
he can afford to let alone.

WALDEN, Chapter II.

🖋 I see that, in my own case, money *might* be of great
service to me, but probably it would not be; for the diffi-
culty now is, that I do not improve my opportunities, and
therefore I am not prepared to have my opportunities increased.

LETTER TO HARRISON BLAKE, February 27, 1853.

🖋 Superfluous wealth can buy superfluities only. Money
is not required to buy one necessary of the soul.

WALDEN, Chapter XVIII.

🖋 If there were one who lived wholly without the use
of money, the State itself would hesitate to demand it of
him. But the rich man—not to make any invidious com-

parison—is always sold to the institution which makes him rich. Absolutely speaking, the more money, the less virtue; for money comes between a man and his objects, and obtains them for him; and it was certainly no great virtue to obtain it. It puts to rest many questions which he would otherwise be taxed to answer; while the only new question which it puts is the hard but superfluous one, how to spend it. Thus his moral ground is taken from under his feet. The opportunities of living are diminished in proportion as what are called the "means" are increased. The best thing a man can do for his culture when he is rich is to endeavor to carry out those schemes which he entertained when he was poor.

CIVIL DISOBEDIENCE.

Remarking to old Mr. B—— the other day on the abundance of apples, "Yes," says he, "and fair as dollars too." That's the kind of beauty they see in apples.

JOURNAL, October 7, 1860.

The problem of life becomes, one cannot say by how many degrees, more complicated as our material wealth is increased—whether that needle they tell of was a gateway or not—since the problem is not merely nor mainly to get life for our bodies, but by this or a similar discipline to get life for our souls; by cultivating the lowland farm on right principles, that is, with this view, to turn it into an upland farm. You have so many more talents to account for. If I accomplish as much more in spiritual work as I am richer in worldly goods, then I am just as worthy, or worth just as much, as I was before, and no more.

LETTER TO HARRISON BLAKE, February 27, 1853.

ON WEALTH

O how I laugh when I think of my vague, indefinite riches. No run on my bank can drain it, for my wealth is not possession but enjoyment.

LETTER TO HARRISON BLAKE, December 6, 1856.

In my experience I have found nothing so truly impoverishing as what is called wealth, i.e. the command of greater means than you had before possessed, though comparatively few and slight still, for you thus inevitably acquire a more expensive habit of living, and even the very same necessaries and comforts cost you more than they once did. Instead of gaining, you have lost some independence, and if your income should be suddenly lessened, you would find yourself poor, though possessed of the same means which once made you rich.

JOURNAL, January 20, 1856.

Merely to come into the world the heir of a fortune is not to be born, but to be still-born, rather. To be supported by the charity of friends, or a government pension —provided you continue to breathe—by whatever fine synonyms you describe these relations, is to go into the almshouse.

LIFE WITHOUT PRINCIPLE.

O solitude! Obscurity! Meanness! I never triumph so as when I have the least success in my neighbor's eyes. The lecturer gets fifty dollars a night; but what becomes of his winter? What consolation will it be hereafter to have fifty thousand dollars for living in the world? I should like not to exchange *any* of my life for money.

LETTER TO HARRISON BLAKE, December 31, 1856.

🖎 Men's minds run so much on work and money that the mass instantly associate all literary labor with a pecuniary reward. They are mainly curious to know how much money the lecturer or author gets for his work. They think that the naturalist takes so much pains to collect plants or animals because he is paid for it. An Irishman who saw me in the fields making a minute in my notebook took it for granted that I was casting up my wages and actually inquired what they came to, as if he had never dreamed of any other use for writing. I might have quoted to him that the wages of sin is death, as the most pertinent answer.

JOURNAL, April 3, 1859.

🖎 When my eye ranges over some thirty miles of this globe's surface—an eminence green and waving, with sky and mountains to bound it—I am richer than Croesus.

JOURNAL, 1850.

🖎 Who will not confess that the necessity to get money has helped to ripen some of his schemes?

JOURNAL, February 6, 1852.

🖎 The less you get, the happier and richer you are. The rich man's son gets cocoanuts, and the poor man's, pignuts; but the worst of it is that the former never goes a-cocoanutting, and so he never gets the cream of the cocoanut as the latter does the cream of the pignut.

JOURNAL, November 28, 1860.

Day and night, summer and winter, sick or well, in war and in peace, men speak of and believe in gold as a great treasure. By a thousand comparisons they prove their devotion to it. If wise men or true philosophers bore any considerable proportion to the whole number of men, gold would be treated with no such distinction. Men seriously and, if possible, religiously believe in and worship gold. They hope to earn golden opinions, to celebrate their golden wedding. They dream of the golden age. Now it is not its intrinsic beauty or value, but its rarity and arbitrarily attached value, that distinguishes gold.

JOURNAL, October 13, 1860.

There is a reptile in the throat of the greedy man always thirsting and famishing. It is not his own natural hunger and thirst which he satisfies.

JOURNAL, September 2, 1851.

I told such a man the other day that I had got a Canada lynx here in Concord, and his instant question was, "Have you got the reward for him?" What reward? Why, the ten dollars which the State offers. As long as I saw him he neither said nor thought anything about the lynx, but only about this reward. You might have inferred that ten dollars was something rarer in his neighborhood than a lynx even, and he was anxious to see it on that account. I have thought that a lynx was a bright-eyed, four-legged, furry beast of the cat kind, very *current*, indeed, though its natural gait is by leaps. But he knew it to be a draught drawn by the cashier of the wildcat bank on the State treasury, payable at sight.

JOURNAL, November 29, 1860.

It is foolish for a man to accumulate material wealth chiefly, houses and land. Our stock in life, our real estate, is that amount of thought which we have had, which we have thought out. The ground we have thus created is forever pasturage for our thoughts. I fall back on to visions which I have had. What else adds to my possessions and makes me rich in all lands? If you have ever done any work with these finest tools, the imagination and fancy and reason, it is a new creation, independent on the world, and a possession forever. You have laid up something against a rainy day. You have to that extent cleared the wilderness.

JOURNAL, May 1, 1857.

That man is the richest whose pleasures are the cheapest.

JOURNAL, March 11, 1856.

On Leisure ❊ ❊

❊ Let us spend one day as deliberately as Nature, and not be thrown off the track by every nutshell and mosquito's wing that falls on the rails.

WALDEN, Chapter II.

❊ A broad margin of leisure is as beautiful in a man's life as in a book.

JOURNAL, December 28, 1852.

❊ All the world complains nowadays of a press of trivial duties and engagements, which prevents their employing themselves on some higher ground they know of; but, undoubtedly, if they were made of the right stuff to work on that higher ground, provided they were released from all those engagements, they would now at once fulfill the superior engagement, and neglect all the rest, as naturally as they breathe. They would never be caught saying that they had no time for this, when the dullest man knows that this is all that he has time for. No man who acts from a sense of duty ever puts the lesser duty above the greater. No man has the desire and the ability to work on high things, but he has also the ability to build himself a high staging.

LETTER TO HARRISON BLAKE, July 21, 1852.

⚜ I love a broad margin to my life. Sometimes, in a summer morning, having taken my accustomed bath, I sat in my sunny doorway from sunrise till noon, rapt in a revery, amidst the pines and hickories and sumachs, in undisturbed solitude and stillness, while the birds sang around or flitted noiseless through the house, until by the sun falling in at my west window, or the noise of some traveller's wagon on the distant highway, I was reminded of the lapse of time. I grew in those seasons like corn in the night, and they were far better than any work of the hands would have been. They were not time substracted from my life, but so much over and above my usual allowance.

WALDEN, Chapter IV.

⚜ Why should we live with such hurry and waste of life? We are determined to be starved before we are hungry. Men say that a stitch in time saves nine, and so they take a thousand stitches today to save nine tomorrow.

WALDEN, Chapter II.

⚜ One little chore to do, one little commission to fulfill, one message to carry, would spoil heaven itself.

JOURNAL, July 21, 1851.

❀ Winter has come unnoticed by me, I have been so busy writing. This is the life most lead in respect to Nature. How different from my habitual one! It is hasty, coarse, and trivial, as if you were a spindle in a factory. The other is leisurely, fine, and glorious, like a flower. In the first case you are merely getting your living; in the second you live as you go along. You travel only on roads of the proper grade without jar or running off the track, and sweep round the hills by beautiful curves.

JOURNAL, December 8, 1854.

❀ Thinking this afternoon of the prospect of my writing lectures and going abroad to read them the next winter, I realize how incomparably great the advantages of obscurity and poverty which I have enjoyed so long (and may still perhaps enjoy). I thought with what more than princely, with what poetical, leisure I had spent my years hitherto, without care or engagement, fancy-free. I have given myself up to nature; I have lived so many springs and summers and autumns and winters as if I had nothing else to do but *live* them, and imbibe whatever nutriment they had for me; I have spent a couple of years, for instance, with the flowers chiefly, having none other so binding engagement as to observe when they opened; I could have afforded to spend a whole fall observing the changing tints of the foliage. Ah, how I have thriven on solitude and poverty! I cannot overstate this advantage. I do not see how I could have enjoyed it, if the public had been expecting as much of me as there is danger now that they will. If I go abroad lecturing, how shall I ever recover the lost winter?

JOURNAL, September 19, 1854.

✵ I have spent many an hour, when I was younger, floating over its surface as the zephyr willed, having paddled my boat to the middle, and lying on my back across the seats, in a summer forenoon, dreaming awake, until I was aroused by the boat touching the sand, and I arose to see what shore my fates had impelled me to; days when idleness was the most attractive and productive industry. Many a forenoon have I stolen away, preferring to spend thus the most valued part of the day; for I was rich, if not in money, in sunny hours and summer days, and spent them lavishly; nor do I regret that I did not waste more of them in the workshop or the teacher's desk.

WALDEN, Chapter IX.

✵ Haste makes waste, no less in life than in housekeeping.

JOURNAL, December 28, 1852.

✵ My days were not days of the week, bearing the stamp of any heathen deity, nor were they minced into hours and fretted by the ticking of a clock; for I lived like the Puri Indians, of whom it is said that "for yesterday, today, and tomorrow they have only one word, and they express the variety of meaning by pointing backward for yesterday, forward for tomorrow, and overhead for the passing day." This was sheer idleness to my fellow-townsmen, no doubt; but if the birds and flowers had tried me by their standard, I should not have been found wanting.

WALDEN, Chapter IV.

74

ON LEISURE

⚜ One moment of life costs many hours, hours not of business but of preparation and invitation. Yet the man who does not betake himself at once and desperately to sawing is called a loafer, though he may be knocking at the doors of heaven all the while, which shall surely be opened to him. That aim in life is highest which requires the highest and finest discipline. How much, what infinite, leisure it requires, as of a lifetime, to appreciate a single phenomenon! You must camp down beside it as for life, having reached your land of promise, and give yourself wholly to it. It must stand for the whole world to you, symbolical of all things.

JOURNAL, December 28, 1852.

⚜ Yet, after all, the truly efficient laborer will not crowd his day with work, but will saunter to his task, surrounded by a wide halo of ease and leisure, and then do but what he loves best. He is anxious only about the fruitful kernels of time. Though the hen should sit all day, she could lay only one egg, and, besides, would not have picked up materials for another. Let a man take time enough for the most trivial deed, though it be but the paring of his nails. The buds swell imperceptibly, without hurry or confusion, as if the short spring days were an eternity.

THE WEEK, Sunday.

⚜ Of all the duties of life it is hardest to be in earnest; it implies a good deal both before and behind. I sit here in the barn this flowing afternoon weather, while the

75

school bell is ringing in the village, and find that all the things immediate to be done are very trivial. I could postpone them to hear this locust sing.

JOURNAL, August 18, 1841.

✿ What are threescore years and ten hurriedly and coarsely lived to moments of divine leisure in which your life is coincident with the life of the universe? We live too fast and coarsely, just as we eat too fast, and do not know the true savor of our food.

JOURNAL, December 28, 1852.

On Government ❈ ❈

❈ Let every man make known what kind of government would command his respect, and that will be one step toward obtaining it.

CIVIL DISOBEDIENCE.

❈ Under a government which imprisons any unjustly, the true place for a just man is also in prison.

CIVIL DISOBEDIENCE.

❈ The ring-leader of the mob will soonest be admitted into the councils of state.

JOURNAL, February 12, 1840.

❈ I heartily accept the motto, "That government is best which governs least;" and I would like to see it acted up to more rapidly and systematically. Carried out, it finally amounts to this, which also I believe— "That government is best which governs not at all;" and when men are prepared for it, that will be the kind of government which they will have.

CIVIL DISOBEDIENCE.

77

THE THOUGHTS OF THOREAU

✗ Politics is, as it were, the gizzard of society, full of grit and gravel, and the two political parties are its two opposite halves, which grind on each other.

JOURNAL, November 10, 1851.

✗ Why will men be such fools as to trust to lawyers for a *moral* reform? I do not believe that there is a judge in this country prepared to decide by the principle that a law is immoral and therefore of no force. They put themselves, or rather are by character, exactly on a level with the marine who discharges his musket in any direction in which he is ordered. They are just as much tools, and as little men.

JOURNAL, June 16, 1854.

✗ Nobody legislates for me, for the way would be not to legislate at all.

JOURNAL, March 23, 1853.

✗ My father asked John Legross if he took an interest in politics and did his duty to his country in this crisis. He said he did. He went into the woodshed and read the newspaper Sundays.

JOURNAL, September 2, 1856.

✗ The fate of the country does not depend on how you vote at the polls—the worst man is as strong as the best at that game; it does not depend on what kind of paper you drop into the ballot-box once a year, but on what kind of man you drop from your chamber into the street every morning.

SLAVERY IN MASSACHUSETTS.

ON GOVERNMENT

꙾ To one who habitually endeavors to contemplate the true state of things, the political state can hardly be said to have any existence whatever. It is unreal, incredible, and insignificant to him, and for him to endeavor to extract the truth from such lean material is like making sugar from linen rags, when sugar-cane may be had.

THE WEEK, Monday.

꙾ Must the citizen ever for a moment, or in the least degree, resign his conscience to the legislator? Why has every man a conscience, then? I think that we should be men first, and subjects afterwards.

CIVIL DISOBEDIENCE.

꙾ I cannot for an instant recognize that political organization as *my* government which is the *slave's* government also.

CIVIL DISOBEDIENCE.

꙾ The mass of men serve the state thus, not as men mainly, but as machines, with their bodies. They are the standing army, and the militia, jailers, constables, *posse comitatus,* etc. In most cases there is no free exercise whatever of the judgment or of the moral sense; but they put themselves on a level with wood and earth and stones; and wooden men can perhaps be manufactured that will serve the purpose as well. Such command no more respect than men of straw or a lump of dirt. They have the same sort of worth only as horses and dogs. Yet such as these even are commonly esteemed good citizens. Others—as most legislators, politicians, lawyers, ministers, and office-holders—serve the state chiefly with their heads; and, as they rarely make any moral distinctions, they are as likely to serve the devil, without *intending* it, as God. A very few—as heroes, patriots, martyrs, reformers in the great sense, and *men*—serve the state with their consciences also, and so necessarily resist it for the most part; and they are commonly treated as enemies by it.

CIVIL DISOBEDIENCE.

The law will never make men free; it is the men who have got to make the law free. They are the lovers of law and order who observe the law when the government breaks it.

SLAVERY IN MASSACHUSETTS.

It is not desirable to cultivate a respect for the law, so much as for the right.

CIVIL DISOBEDIENCE.

Law never made men a whit more just; and, by means of their respect for it, even the well-disposed are daily made the agents of injustice.

CIVIL DISOBEDIENCE.

I do not wish to quarrel with any man or nation. I do not wish to split hairs, to make fine distinctions, or set myself up as better than my neighbors. I seek rather, I may say, even an excuse for conforming to the laws of the land.

CIVIL DISOBEDIENCE.

The authority of government, even such as I am willing to submit to—for I will cheerfully obey those who know and can do better than I, and in many things even those who neither know nor can do so well—is still an impure one: to be strictly just, it must have the sanction and consent of the governed. It can have no pure right over my person and property but what I concede to it.

CIVIL DISOBEDIENCE.

I have never declined paying the highway tax, because I am as desirous of being a good neighbor as I am of being a bad subject; and as for supporting schools, I am doing my part to educate my fellow-countrymen now. It is for no particular item in the tax-bill that I refuse to pay it. I simply wish to refuse allegiance to the State, to withdraw and stand aloof from it effectually. I do not care to trace the course of my dollar, if I could, till it buys a man or a musket to shoot one with—the dollar is innocent—but I am concerned to trace the effects of my allegiance.

CIVIL DISOBEDIENCE.

I quarrel not with far-off foes, but with those who, near at home, cooperate with, and do the bidding of, those far away, and without whom the latter would be harmless.

CIVIL DISOBEDIENCE.

I please myself with imagining a State at last which can afford to be just to all men, and to treat the individual with respect as a neighbor; which even would not think it inconsistent with its own repose if a few men were to

81

live aloof from it, not meddling with it, nor embraced by it, who fulfilled all the duties of neighbors and fellowmen.

CIVIL DISOBEDIENCE.

⚔ I have contemplated the imprisonment of the offender, rather than the seizure of his goods—though both will serve the same purpose—because they who assert the purest right, and consequently are most dangerous to a corrupt State, commonly have not spent much time in accumulating property.

CIVIL DISOBEDIENCE.

⚔ The poor President, what with preserving his popularity and doing his duty, does not know what to do.

JOURNAL, November 17, 1850.

⚔ If we were left solely to the wordy wit of legislators in Congress for our guidance, uncorrected by the seasonable experience and the effectual complaints of the people, America would not long retain her front rank among the nations.

CIVIL DISOBEDIENCE.

⚔ Trade and commerce, if they were not made of india-rubber, would never manage to bounce over the obstacles which legislators are continually putting in their way; and, if one were to judge these men wholly by the effects of their actions and not partly by their intentions, they would deserve to be classed and punished with those mischievous persons who put obstructions on the railroads.

CIVIL DISOBEDIENCE.

ON GOVERNMENT

I cannot take up a newspaper but I find that some wretched government or other, hard pushed and on its last legs, is interceding with me, the reader, to vote for it—more importunate than an Italian beggar.

JOURNAL, November 17, 1850.

The progress from an absolute to a limited monarchy, from a limited monarchy to a democracy, is a progress toward a true respect for the individual.

CIVIL DISOBEDIENCE.

What makes the United States government, on the whole, more tolerable—I mean for us lucky white men— is the fact that there is so much less government with us.

A YANKEE IN CANADA.

The effect of a good government is to make life more valuable—of a bad government, to make it less valuable. We can afford that railroad and all merely material stock should depreciate, for that only compels us to live more simply and economically; but suppose the value of life itself should be depreciated.

JOURNAL, June 16, 1854.

That certainly is the best government where the inhabitants are least often reminded of the government.

JOURNAL, August 21, 1851.

On Day and Night ✻ ✻

✻ Morning brings back the heroic ages.

WALDEN, Chapter II.

✻ Morning is when I am awake and there is a dawn in me.

WALDEN, Chapter II.

✻ To see the sun rise and go down every day would preserve us sane forever—so to relate ourselves, for our mind's and body's health, to a universal fact.

JOURNAL, January 20, 1852

✻ Morning air! If men will not drink of this at the fountain-head of the day, why, then, we must even bottle up some and sell it in the shops, for the benefit of those who have lost their subscription ticket to morning time in this world.

WALDEN, Chapter V.

ON DAY AND NIGHT

❊ It is day, and we have more of that same light that the moon sent us, but not reflected now, but shining directly. The sun is a fuller moon. Who knows how much lighter day there may be?

JOURNAL, June 12, 1852.

❊ The day is an epitome of the year. The night is the winter, the morning and evening are the spring and fall, and the noon is the summer.

WALDEN, Chapter XVII.

❊ Would you see your mind, look at the sky. Would you know your own moods, be weather-wise. He whom the weather disappoints, disappoints himself.

JOURNAL, January 26, 1852.

❊ How soon the sun gets above the hills, as if he would accomplish his whole diurnal journey in a few hours at this rate! But it is a long way round, and these are nothing to the hill of heaven.

JOURNAL, November 7, 1853.

❊ The voice of the cricket, heard at noon from deep in the grass, allies day to night. It is unaffected by sun and moon. It is a midnight sound heard at noon, a midday sound heard at midnight.

JOURNAL, June 29, 1851.

❊ The morning hope is soon lost in what becomes the routine of the day, and we do not recover ourselves again until we land on the pensive shores of evening, shores which skirt the great western continent of the night.

JOURNAL, January 8, 1854.

❋ How swiftly the earth appears to revolve at sunset, which at midday appears to rest on its axle.

JOURNAL, December 21, 1851.

❋ We never tire of the drama of sunset. I go forth each afternoon and look into the west a quarter of an hour before sunset, with fresh curiosity, to see what new picture will be painted there, what new phenomena exhibited, what new dissolving views. Can Washington Street or Broadway show anything as good? Every day a new picture is painted and framed, held up for half an hour, in such lights as the Great Artist chooses, and then withdrawn, and the curtain falls.

JOURNAL, January 7, 1852.

❋ The man is blessed who every day is permitted to behold anything so pure and serene as the western sky at sunset, while revolutions vex the world.

JOURNAL, December 27, 1851.

❋ If I were to choose a time for a friend to make a passing visit to this world for the first time, in the full possession of all his faculties, perchance it would be at a moment when the sun was setting with splendor in the west, his light reflected far and wide through the clarified air after a rain, and a brilliant rainbow, as now, o'erarching the eastern sky.

JOURNAL, August 7, 1852.

❋ There are meteorologists, but who keeps a record of the fairer sunsets? While men are recording the direction of the wind, they neglect to record the beauty of the sunset or the rainbow.

JOURNAL, June 28, 1852.

ON DAY AND NIGHT

❋ As the skies appear to a man, so is his mind. Some see only clouds there; some, prodigies and portents; some rarely look up at all; their heads, like the brutes', are directed toward earth. Some behold there serenity, purity, beauty ineffable. The world run to see the panorama, when there is a panorama in the sky which few go out to see.

JOURNAL, January 17, 1852.

❋ Every sunset which I witness inspires me with the desire to go to a West as distant and as fair as that into which the sun goes down. He appears to migrate westward daily, and tempt us to follow him. He is the Great Western Pioneer whom the nations follow.

WALKING.

❋ Clouds are our mountains, and the child who had lived in a plain always and had never seen a mountain would find that he was prepared for the sight of them by his familiarity with clouds.

JOURNAL, January 14, 1852.

❋ In proportion as I have celestial thoughts, is the necessity for me to be out and behold the western sky before sunset these winter days. That is the symbol of the unclouded mind that knows neither winter nor summer.

JOURNAL, January 17, 1852.

❋ Is not the dew but a humbler, gentler rain, the nightly rain, above which we raise our heads and unobstructedly behold the stars? The mountains are giants which tower above the rain, as we do above the dew in the grass; it only wets their feet.

JOURNAL, November 21, 1853.

❋ When I consider how, after sunset, the stars come out gradually in troops from behind the hills and woods, I confess that I could not have contrived a more curious and inspiring night.

JOURNAL, July 26, 1840.

❋ So is not shade as good as sunshine, night as day? Why be eagles and thrushes always, and owls and whip-poor-wills never?

JOURNAL, June 16, 1840.

❋ As the twilight deepens and the moonlight is more and more bright, I begin to distinguish myself, who I am and where; as my walls contract, I become more collected and composed, and sensible of my own existence, as when a lamp is brought into a dark apartment and I see who the company are.

JOURNAL, August 5, 1851.

❋ By moonlight all is simple. We are enabled to erect ourselves, our minds, on account of the fewness of objects. We are no longer distracted. It is simple as bread and water. It is simple as the rudiments of an art—a lesson to be taken before sunlight, perchance, to prepare us for that.

JOURNAL, September 22, 1854.

❋ Nature seems not to have designed that man should be much abroad by night, and in the moon proportioned the light fitly. By the faintness and rareness of the light compared to that of the sun, she expresses her intention with regard to him.

JOURNAL, June 14, 1851.

ON DAY AND NIGHT

✳ Only the Hunter's and Harvest moons are famous, but I think that each full moon deserves to be and has its own character well marked. One might be called the Midsummer-Night Moon.

JOURNAL, June 11, 1851.

✳ When man is asleep and day fairly forgotten, then is the beauty of moonlight seen over lonely pastures where cattle are silently feeding.

JOURNAL, June 14, 1851.

✳ I saw a distant river by moonlight, making no noise, yet flowing, as by day, still to the sea, like melted silver reflecting the moonlight. Far away it lay encircling the earth. How far away it may look in the night, and even from a low hill how miles away down in the valley! As far off as paradise and the delectable country! There is a certain glory attends on water by night. By it the heavens are related to the earth, undistinguishable from a sky beneath you.

JOURNAL, June 13, 1851.

✳ When I am outside, on the outskirts of the town, enjoying the still majesty of the moon, I am wont to think that all men are aware of this miracle, that they too are silently worshipping this manifestation of divinity elsewhere. But when I go into the house I am undeceived; they are absorbed in checkers or chess or novel, though they may have been advertised of the brightness through the shutters.

JOURNAL, May 16, 1851.

89

✳ If there is nothing new on earth, still there is something new in the heavens. We have always a resource in the skies. They are constantly turning a new page to view. The wind sets the types in this blue ground, and the inquiring may always read a new truth.

JOURNAL, November 17, 1837.

✳ Men attach a false importance to celestial phenomena as compared with terrestrial, as if it were more respectable and elevating to watch your neighbors than to mind your own affairs.

JOURNAL, October 16, 1859.

✳ Is not the midnight like Central Africa to most of us? Are we not tempted to explore it—to penetrate to the shores of Lake Tchad, and discover the source of its Nile, perchance the Mountains of the Moon?

NIGHT AND MOONLIGHT.

✳ The stars are the apexes of what wonderful triangles! What distant and different beings in the various mansions of the universe are contemplating the same one at the same moment!

WALDEN, Chapter I.

✳ If the day and the night are such that you greet them with joy, and life emits a fragrance like flowers and sweet-scented herbs, is more elastic, more starry, more immortal—that is your success.

WALDEN, Chapter XI.

On Science ⚘ ⚘

⚘ Science suggests the value of mutual intelligence.
JOURNAL, January 15, 1853.

⚘ Science never saw a ghost, nor does it look for any, but it sees everywhere the traces, as it is itself the agent, of a Universal Intelligence.
JOURNAL, December 1, 1853.

⚘ How little I know of that *arbor-vitae* when I have learned only what science can tell me! It is but a word. It is not a *tree* of *life*.
JOURNAL, March 5, 1858.

⚘ The knowledge of an unlearned man is living and luxuriant like a forest, but covered with mosses and lichens and for the most part inaccessible and going to waste; the knowledge of the man of science is like timber collected in yards for public works, which still supports a green sprout here and there, but even this is liable to dry rot.

JOURNAL, January 7, 1851.

✍ I am constantly assisted by the books in identifying a particular plant and learning some of its humbler uses, but I rarely read a sentence in a botany which reminds me of flowers or living plants. Very few indeed write as if they had seen the thing which they pretend to describe.

JOURNAL, September 22, 1860.

✍ Lichens, which are so thin, are described in the *dry* state, as they are most commonly, not most truly, seen. Truly, they are *dryly* described.

JOURNAL, March 23, 1853.

✍ Modern botanical descriptions approach ever nearer to the dryness of an algebraic formula, as if $x + y$ were $=$ to a love-letter. It is the keen joy and discrimination of the child who has just seen a flower for the first time and comes running in with it to its friends. How much better to describe your object in fresh English words rather than in these conventional Latinisms!

JOURNAL, December 16, 1859.

✍ To Cambridge, where I read in Gerard's Herbal. His admirable though quaint descriptions are, to my mind, greatly superior to the modern more scientific ones. He describes not according to rule but to his natural delight in the plants. He brings them vividly before you, as one who has seen and delighted in them. It is almost as good as to see the plants themselves. It suggests that we cannot too often get rid of the barren assumption that is in our science. His leaves are leaves; his flowers, flowers; his fruit, fruit. They are green and colored and fragrant. It is a man's knowledge added to a child's delight.

JOURNAL, December 16, 1859.

If there is not something mystical in your explanation, something unexplainable to the understanding, some elements of mystery, it is quite insufficient. If there is nothing in it which speaks to my imagination, what boots it? What sort of science is it which enriches the understanding, but robs the imagination? Not merely robs Peter to pay Paul, but takes from Peter more than it ever gives to Paul?

JOURNAL, December 25, 1851.

The old naturalists were so sensitive and sympathetic to nature that they could be surprised by the ordinary events of life. It was an incessant miracle to them, and therefore gorgons and flying dragons were not incredible to them. The greatest and saddest defect is not credulity, but our habitual forgetfulness that our science is ignorance.

JOURNAL, March 5, 1860.

One studies books of science merely to learn the language of naturalists—to be able to communicate with them.

JOURNAL, March 23, 1853.

✒ I look over the report of the doings of a scientific association and am surprised that there is so little life to be reported; I am put off with a parcel of dry technical terms. Anything living is easily and naturally expressed in popular language. I cannot help suspecting that the life of these learned professors has been almost as inhuman and wooden as a rain-gauge or self-registering magnetic machine. They communicate no fact which rises to the temperature of blood-heat. It doesn't all amount to one rhyme.

JOURNAL, May 6, 1854.

✒ Though science may sometimes compare herself to a child picking up pebbles on the seashore, that is a rare mood with her; ordinarily her practical belief is that it is only a few pebbles which are *not* known, weighed and measured. A new species of fish signifies hardly more than a new name. See what is contributed in the scientific reports. One counts the fin-rays, another measures the intestines, a third daguerreotypes a scale, etc., etc., otherwise there's nothing to be said. As if all but this were done, and these were very rich and generous contributions to science. Her votaries may be seen wandering along the shore of the ocean of truth, with their backs to that ocean, ready to seize on the shells which are cast up. You would say that the scientific bodies were terribly put to it for objects and subjects. A dead specimen of an animal, if it is only well preserved in alcohol, is just as good for science as a living one preserved in its native element.

JOURNAL, November 30, 1858.

ON SCIENCE

🖋 Science in many departments of natural history does not pretend to go beyond the shell, i.e., it does not get to animated nature at all. A history of animated nature must itself be animated.

JOURNAL, February 18, 1860.

🖋 A description of animals, too, from a dead specimen only, as if, in a work on man, you were to describe a dead man only, omitting his manners and customs, his institutions and divine faculties, from want of opportunity to observe them, suggesting, perchance, that the colors of the eye are said to be much more brilliant in the living specimen, and that some cannibal, your neighbor, who has tried him on his table, has found him to be sweet and nutritious, good on the gridiron. Having no opportunity to observe his habits, because you do not live in the country. Only dindons and dandies. Nothing is known of his habits. Food: seeds of wheat, beef, pork, and potatoes.

JOURNAL, March 22, 1853.

🖋 As it is important to consider Nature from the point of view of science, remembering the nomenclature and system of men, and so, if possible, go a step further in that direction, so it is equally important often to ignore or forget all that men presume that they know, and take an original and unprejudiced view of Nature, letting her make what impression she will on you, as the first men, and all children and natural men still do. For our science, so called, is always more barren and mixed up with error than our sympathies are.

JOURNAL, February 28, 1860.

🖋 All science is only a makeshift, a means to an end which is never attained.

JOURNAL, October 13, 1860.

🖋 I feel, of course, very ignorant in a museum. I know nothing about the things which they have there—no more than I should know my friends in the tomb. I walk amid those jars of bloated creatures which they label frogs, a total stranger, without the least froggy thought being suggested. Not one of them can croak. They leave behind all life they that enter there, both frogs and men.

JOURNAL, February 18, 1860.

On Friendship ❀ ❀

❀ You may buy a servant or slave, in short, but you cannot buy a friend.

JOURNAL, November 28, 1860.

❀ A man cannot be said to succeed in this life who does not satisfy one friend.

JOURNAL, February 19, 1857.

❀ A Friend is one who incessantly pays us the compliment of expecting from us all the virtues, and who can appreciate them in us. It takes two to speak the truth—one to speak and another to hear.

THE WEEK, Wednesday.

❀ On the death of a friend, we should consider that the fates through confidence have devolved on us the task of a double living, that we have henceforth to fulfill the promise of our friend's life also, in our own, to the world.

JOURNAL, February 28, 1840.

97

❀ The obstacles which the heart meets with are like granite blocks which one alone cannot move.

JOURNAL, October 27, 1851.

❀ To one we love we are related as to nature in the spring. Our dreams are mutually intelligible. We take the census, and find there is one.

JOURNAL, April 30, 1851.

❀ Some men may be my acquaintances merely, but one whom I have been accustomed to regard, to idealize, to have dreams about as a friend, and mix up intimately with myself, can never degenerate into an acquaintance. I must know him on that higher ground or not know him at all.

JOURNAL, November 24, 1850.

❀ If I had never thought of you as a friend, I could make much use of you as an acquaintance.

JOURNAL, January 31, 1852.

❀ What if we feel a yearning to which no breast answers? I walk alone. My heart is full. Feelings impede the current of my thoughts. I knock on the earth for my friend. I expect to meet him at every turn; but no friend appears, and perhaps none is dreaming of me. I am tired of frivolous society, in which silence is forever the most natural and the best manners. I would fain walk on the deep waters, but my companions will only walk on shallows and puddles. I am naturally silent in the midst of twenty from day to day, from year to year. I am rarely reminded of their presence. Two yards of politeness do not make society for me. One complains that I do not take his jokes. I took them before he had done uttering them, and went my way. One talks to me of his apples and pears, and I depart with my secret untold. His are not the apples that tempt me.

JOURNAL, June 11, 1855.

❀ I have some good friends from whom I am wont to part with disappointment, for they neither care what I think nor mind what I say. The greatest compliment that was ever paid me was when one asked me what I *thought,* and attended to my answer.

JOURNAL, January 27, 1854.

❀ In what concerns you much, do not think that you have companions: know that you are alone in the world.

LETTER TO HARRISON BLAKE, March 27, 1848.

❀ It often happens that a man is more humanely related to a cat or dog than to any human being.

JOURNAL, April 29, 1851.

❀ Often, I would rather undertake to shoulder a barrel of pork and carry it a mile than take into my company a man. It would not be so heavy a weight upon my mind. I could put it down and only feel my *back* ache for it.

JOURNAL, August 31, 1856.

❀ Woe to him who wants a companion, for he is unfit to be the companion even to himself.

JOURNAL, June, 1850.

❧ There are enough who will flatter me with sweet words, and anon use bitter ones to balance them, but they are not my friends. Simple sincerity and truth are rare indeed.

JOURNAL, September 9, 1852.

❧ We love to talk with those who can make a good guess at us, not with those who talk to us as if we were somebody else all the while.

JOURNAL, September 9, 1852.

❧ I have never met with a friend who furnished me sea-room. I have only tacked a few times and come to anchor —not sailed—made no voyage, carried no venture.

JOURNAL, August 24, 1852.

❧ My friend is one whom I meet, who takes me for what I am. A stranger takes me for something else than I am. We do not speak, we cannot communicate, till we find that we are recognized. The stranger supposes in our stead a third person whom we do not know, and we leave him to converse with that one. It is suicide for us to become abetters in misapprehending ourselves. Suspicion creates the stranger and substitutes him for the friend. I cannot abet any man in misapprehending myself.

JOURNAL, October 23, 1852.

❧ If my friend would take a quarter part the pains to show me himself that he does to show me a piece of roast beef, I should feel myself irresistibly invited.

JOURNAL, May 19, 1856.

ON FRIENDSHIP

❦ Who are the estranged? Two friends explaining.
JOURNAL, December 21, 1851.

❦ I never realized so distinctly as this moment that I am peacefully parting company with the best friend I ever had, by each pursuing his proper path. I perceive that it is possible that we may have a better *understanding* now than when we were more at one. Not expecting such essential agreement as before. Simply our paths diverge.
JOURNAL, January 21, 1852.

❦ How can they keep together who are going different ways?
JOURNAL, July 12, 1851.

❦ I know but one with whom I can walk, I might as well be sitting in a bar-room with them as walk and talk with most. We are never side by side in our thoughts, and we cannot hear each other's silence. Indeed, we cannot be silent. We are forever breaking silence, that is all, and mending nothing.
JOURNAL, July 12, 1851.

❦ To attain to a true relation to one human creature is enough to make a year memorable.
JOURNAL, March 30, 1851.

❦ Friendship is the fruit which the year should bear; it lends its fragrance to the flowers, and it is in vain if we get only a large crop of apples without it.
JOURNAL, July 13, 1857.

❦   The Friend is some fair floating isle of palms eluding the mariner in Pacific seas. Many are the dangers to be encountered, equinoctial gales and coral reefs, ere he may sail before the constant trades. But who would not sail through mutiny and storm, even over Atlantic waves, to reach the fabulous retreating shores of some continent man?

THE WEEK, Wednesday.

❦   Ah, my friends, I know you better than you think, and love you better, too. The day after never, we will have an explanation.

JOURNAL, November 8, 1857.

On Birds 🐦 🐦

🐦 A man's interest in a single bluebird is worth more than a complete but dry list of the fauna and flora of a town.

LETTER TO DANIEL RICKETSON, November 22, 1858.

🐦 All that was ripest and fairest in the wilderness and the wild man is preserved and transmitted to us in the strain of the wood thrush.

JOURNAL, June 22, 1853.

🐦 I once had a sparrow alight upon my shoulder for a moment while I was hoeing in a village garden, and I felt that I was more distinguished by that circumstance than I should have been by any epaulet I could have worn.

WALDEN, Chapter XV.

He who cuts down woods beyond a certain limit exterminates birds.

JOURNAL, May 17, 1853.

I heard a robin in the distance, the first I had heard for many a thousand years, methought, whose note I shall not forget for many a thousand more—the same sweet and powerful song as of yore. O the evening robin, at the end of a New England summer day! If I could ever find the twig he sits upon! I mean *he;* I mean *the twig.*

WALDEN, Chapter XVII.

The bluebird carries the sky on his back.

JOURNAL, April 3, 1852.

The first sparrow of spring! The year beginning with younger hope than ever! The faint silvery warblings heard over the partially bare and moist fields from the bluebird, the song sparrow, and the red-wing, as if the last flakes of winter tinkled as they fell! What at such a time are histories, chronologies, traditions, and all written revelations?

WALDEN, Chapter XVII.

How much more habitable a few birds make the fields! At the end of winter, when the fields are bare and there is nothing to relieve the monotony of the withered vegetation, our life seems reduced to its lowest terms. But let a bluebird come and warble over them, and what a change!

JOURNAL, March 18, 1858.

night I heard them here. They go honking over cities where the arts flourish, waking the inhabitants; over Statehouses and capitols, where legislatures sit; over harbors where fleets lie at anchor; mistaking the city, perhaps, for a swamp or the edge of a lake, about settling in it, not suspecting that greater geese than they have settled there.

JOURNAL, December 13, 1855.

As I flounder along the Corner road against the root fence, a very large flock of snow buntings alight with a wheeling flight amid the weeds rising above the snow in Potter's heater piece—a hundred or two of them. What independent creatures! They go seeking their food from north to south. If New Hampshire or Maine are covered deeply with snow, they scale down to Massachusetts for their breakfasts. Not liking the grain in this field, away they dash to another distant one, attracted by the weeds rising above the snow. Who can guess in what field, by what river or mountain they breakfasted this morning.

JOURNAL, January 21, 1857.

The bluebird on the apple tree, warbling so innocently to inquire if any of its mates are within call—the angel of the spring! Fair and innocent, yet the offspring of the earth. The color of the sky above and of the subsoil beneath. Suggesting what sweet and innocent melody (terrestrial melody) may have its birthplace between the sky and the ground.

JOURNAL, March 10, 1859.

The bluebird which some woodchopper or inspired walker is said to have seen in that sunny interval between the snowstorms is like a speck of clear blue sky seen near the end of a storm, reminding us of an ethereal region and a heaven which we had forgotten. Princes and magistrates are often styled serene, but what is their turbid serenity to that ethereal serenity which the bluebird embodies? His Most Serene Birdship! His soft warble melts in the ear, as the snow is melting in the valleys around. The bluebird comes and with his warble drills the ice and sets free the rivers and ponds and frozen ground. As the sand flows down the slopes a little way, assuming the forms of foliage where the frost comes out of the ground, so this little rill of melody flows a short way down the concave of the sky. The sharp whistle of the blackbird, too, is heard like single sparks or a shower of them shot up from the swamps and seen against the dark winter in the rear.

JOURNAL, March 2, 1859.

Crows will often come flying much out of their way to caw at me.

JOURNAL, November 18, 1857.

Undoubtedly the geese fly more numerously over rivers which, like ours, flow northeasterly—are more at home with the water under them. Each flock runs the gantlet of a thousand gunners, and when you see them steer off from you and your boat you may remember how great their experience in such matters may be, how many

such boats and gunners they have seen and avoided between here and Mexico, and even now, perchance
(though you, low plodding, little dream of it), they see
one or two more lying in wait ahead. They have an experienced ranger of the air for their guide. The echo of
one gun hardly dies away before they see another pointed
at them. How many bullets or smaller shot have sped in
vain toward their ranks!

JOURNAL, March 28, 1859.

🐦 I hear the note of a bobolink concealed in the top of
an apple tree behind me. He is just touching the strings
of his theorbo, his glassicord, his water organ, and one
or two notes globe themselves and fall in liquid bubbles
from his teeming throat. It is as if he touched his harp
within a vase of liquid melody, and when he lifted it out,
the notes fell like bubbles from the trembling strings. Methinks they are the most *liquidly* sweet and melodious
sounds I ever heard. They are refreshing to my ear as the
first distant tinkling and gurgling of a rill to a thirsty man.

JOURNAL, June 1, 1857.

🐦 A child asked concerning a bobolink, "What makes
he sing so sweet, Mother? Do he eat flowers?"

JOURNAL, June 20, 1857.

🐦 What a perfectly New England sound is this voice
of the crow! If you stand perfectly still anywhere in the
outskirts of the town and listen, stilling the almost incessant hum of your own personal factory, this is perhaps
the sound which you will be most sure to hear rising

above all sounds of human industry and leading your thoughts to some far bay in the woods where the crow is venting his disgust. This bird sees the white man come and the Indian withdraw, but it withdraws not. Its untamed voice is still heard above the tinkling of the forge. It sees a race pass away, but it passes not away. It remains to remind us of aboriginal nature.

JOURNAL, March 4, 1859.

What a pity our yard was made so tidy in the fall with rake and fire, and we have now no tall crop of weeds rising above this snow to invite these birds!

JOURNAL, January 6, 1856.

As I come over the hill, I hear the wood thrush singing his evening lay. This is the only bird whose note affects me like music, affects the flow and tenor of my thought, my fancy and imagination. It lifts and exhilarates me. It is inspiring. It is a medicative draught to my soul. It is an elixir to my eyes and a fountain of youth to all my senses. It changes all hours to an eternal morning.

JOURNAL, June 22, 1853.

The thrush alone declares the immortal wealth and vigor that is in the forest. Here is a bird in whose strain the story is told, though Nature waited for the science of aesthetics to discover it to man. Whenever a man hears it, he is young, and Nature is in her spring. Most other birds sing from the level of my ordinary cheerful hours— a carol; but this bird never fails to speak to me out of an ether purer than that I breathe, of immortal beauty and vigor. He deepens the significance of all things seen in the light of his strain. He sings to make men take higher and truer views of things. He sings to amend their institutions; to relieve the slave on the plantation and the prisoner in his dungeon, the slave in the house of luxury and the prisoner of his own low thoughts.

JOURNAL, July 5, 1852.

When we have experienced many disappointments, such as the loss of friends, the notes of birds cease to affect us as they did.

JOURNAL, February 5, 1859.

I hear part of a phoebe's strain, as I go over the railroad bridge. It is the voice of dying summer.

JOURNAL, August 26, 1854.

The tinkling notes of goldfinches and bobolinks which we hear nowadays are of one character and peculiar to the season. They are not voluminous flowers, but rather nuts, of sound—ripened seeds of sound. It is the tinkling of ripened grains in Nature's basket.

JOURNAL, August 10, 1854.

Would it not be well to carry a spy-glass in order to watch these shy birds such as ducks and hawks? In some respects, methinks, it would be better than a gun. The latter brings them nearer dead, but the former alive. You can identify the species better by killing the bird, because it was a dead specimen that was so minutely described, but you can study the habits and appearance best in the living specimen.

JOURNAL, March 29, 1853.

Birds certainly are afraid of man. They allow all other creatures—cows and horses, etc.—excepting only one or two kinds, birds or beasts of prey, to come near them, but not man. What does this fact signify? Does it not signify that man, too, is a beast of prey to them? Is he, then, a true lord of creation, whose subjects are afraid of him, and with reason? They know very well that he is not humane, as he pretends to be.

JOURNAL, October 22, 1855.

Saw a tanager in Sleepy Hollow. It most takes the eye of any bird. You here have the red-wing reversed— the deepest scarlet of the red-wing spread over the whole body, not on the wing-coverts merely, while the wings are black. It flies through the green foliage as if it would ignite the leaves.

JOURNAL, May 20, 1853.

As it grew darker, I was startled by the honking of geese flying low over the woods, like weary travelers getting in late from Southern lakes, and indulging at last in unrestrained complaint and mutual consolation. Standing at my door, I could hear the rush of their wings; when, driving toward my house, they suddenly spied my light, and with hushed clamor wheeled and settled in the pond. So I came in, and shut the door, and passed my first spring night in the woods.

WALDEN, Chapter XVII.

On News ✵ ✵

✵ The newspapers are the ruling power. What Congress does is an afterclap.

JOURNAL, November 17, 1850.

✵ Hardly a man takes a half-hour's nap after dinner, but when he wakes he holds up his head and asks, "What's the news?" as if the rest of mankind had stood his sentinels. Some give directions to be waked every half-hour, doubtless for no other purpose; and then, to pay for it, they tell what they have dreamed. After a night's sleep the news is as indispensable as the breakfast. "Pray tell me anything new that has happened to a man anywhere on this globe"—and he reads it over his coffee and rolls, that a man has had his eyes gouged out this morning on the Wachito River; never dreaming the while that he lives in the dark unfathomed mammoth cave of this world, and has but the rudiment of an eye himself.

WALDEN, Chapter II.

⚘ If words were invented to conceal thought, I think that newspapers are a great improvement on a bad invention. Do not suffer your life to be taken by newspapers.

LETTER TO HARRISON BLAKE, November 20, 1849.

⚘ The newspaper is a Bible which we read every morning and every afternoon, standing and sitting, riding and walking. It is a Bible which every man carries in his pocket, which lies on every table and counter, and which the mail, and thousands of missionaries, are continually dispersing. It is, in short, the only book which America has printed, and which America reads. So wide is its influence. The editor is a preacher whom you voluntarily support. Your tax is commonly one cent daily, and it costs nothing for pew hire. But how many of these preachers preach the truth?

SLAVERY IN MASSACHUSETTS.

⚘ Generally speaking, the political news, whether domestic or foreign, might be written today for the next ten years with sufficient accuracy.

THE WEEK, Monday.

⚘ I am sure that I never read any memorable news in a newspaper. If we read of one man robbed, or murdered, or killed by accident, or one house burned, or one vessel wrecked, or one steamboat blown up, or one cow run over on the Western Railroad, or one mad dog killed, or one lot of grasshoppers in the winter—we never need to read of another. One is enough. If you are acquainted with the principle, what do you care for a myriad instances and applications?

WALDEN, Chapter II.

⚘ It is surprising what a tissue of trifles and crudities make the daily news. For one event of interest there are nine hundred and ninety-nine insignificant, but about the same stress is laid on the last as the first.

JOURNAL, August 9, 1858.

⚘ I have no time to read newspapers. If you chance to live and move and have your being in that thin stratum in which the events which make the news transpire— thinner than the paper on which it is printed—then these things will fill the world for you; but if you soar above or dive below that plane, you cannot remember nor be reminded of them.

JOURNAL, April 3, 1853.

⚘ As for the herd of newspapers, I do not chance to know one in the country that will deliberately print anything that will ultimately and permanently reduce the number of its subscribers.

JOURNAL, October 19, 1859.

⚘ We rarely meet a man who can tell us any news which he has not read in a newspaper, or been told by his neighbor; and, for the most part, the only difference between us and our fellow is that he has seen the newspaper, or been out to tea, and we have not.

LIFE WITHOUT PRINCIPLE.

⚶ There is not a popular magazine in this country that would dare print a child's thought on important subjects without comment. It must be submitted to the D.D.'s. I would it were the chickadee-dees.

LIFE WITHOUT PRINCIPLE.

On Sounds and Silence ❊ ❊

❊ You cannot hear music and noise at the same time.
JOURNAL, April 27, 1854.

❊ Listen to music religiously, as if it were the last strain
you might hear.
JOURNAL, June 12, 1851.

❊ The music of all creatures has to do with their loves,
even of toads and frogs. Is it not the same with man?
JOURNAL, May 6, 1852.

❊ What is the singing of birds, or any natural sound,
compared with the voice of one we love?
JOURNAL, April 30, 1851.

I used to strike with a paddle on the side of my boat on Walden Pond, filling the surrounding woods with circling and dilating sound, awakening the woods, "stirring them up," as a keeper of a menagerie his lions and tigers, a growl from all. All melody is a sweet echo, as it were coincident with the movement of our organs. We wake the echo of the place we are in, its slumbering music.

JOURNAL, 1850.

I should think that savages would have made a god of echo.

JOURNAL, 1850.

Debauched and worn-out senses require the violent vibrations of an instrument to excite them, but *sound* and still youthful senses, not enervated by luxury, hear music in the wind and rain and running water. One would think from reading the critics that music was intermittent as a spring in the desert, depending on some Paganini or Mozart, or heard only when the Pierians or Euterpeans drive through the villages; but music is perpetual, and only hearing is intermittent.

JOURNAL, February 8, 1857.

I hear no sound of a bird as I go up the back road; only a few faint crickets to be heard—these are the birds we are reduced to. What a puny sound this for the great globe to make!

JOURNAL, October 28, 1852.

Only in their saner moments do men hear the crickets. It is balm to the philosopher. It tempers his thoughts. They dwell forever in a temperate latitude. By listening to whom, all voices are tuned. In their song they ignore our accidents. They are not concerned about the news. A quire has begun which pauses not for any news, for it knows only the eternal.

JOURNAL, May 22, 1854.

The earth-song of the cricket! Before Christianity was, it is. Health! health! health! is the burden of its song. When we hear that sound of the crickets in the sod, the world is not so much with us.

JOURNAL, June 17, 1852.

There is something in the music of the cow-bell, something sweeter and more nutritious, than in the milk which the farmers drink.

JOURNAL, June 22, 1853.

There is a cool and breezy south wind, and the ring of the first toad leaks into the general stream of sound, unnoticed by most, as the mill-brook empties into the river and the voyager cannot tell if he is above or below its mouth. The bell was ringing for town meeting, and everyone heard it, but none heard this older and more universal bell, rung by more native Americans all the land over.

JOURNAL, May 1, 1857.

119

✻ I hear faintly the cawing of a crow far, far away, echoing from some unseen woodside, as if deadened by the spring-like vapor which the sun is drawing from the ground. It mingles with the slight murmur of the village, the sound of children at play, as one stream empties gently into another, the wild and the tame are one. What a delicious sound! It is not merely crow calling to crow, for it speaks to me too. I am part of one great creature with him; if he has voice, I have ears. I can hear when he calls, and have engaged not to shoot nor stone him if he will caw to me each spring. On the one hand, it may be, is the sound of children saying their a, b, ab's; on the other, far in the wood-fringed horizon, the cawing of crows from their blessed eternal vacation, out at their long recess, children who have got dismissed!

JOURNAL, January 12, 1855.

✻ The ringing of the church bell is a much more melodious sound than any that is heard within the church.

JOURNAL, January 2, 1842.

✻ As I stand listening for the wren, and sweltering in my greatcoat, I hear the woods filled with the hum of insects, as if my hearing were affected; and thus the summer's quire begins. The silent spaces have begun to be filled with notes of birds and insects and the peep and croak and snore of frogs, even as living green blades are everywhere pushing up amid the sere ones.

JOURNAL, April 25, 1854.

ON SOUNDS AND SILENCE

❊ The whistle of the locomotive penetrates my woods summer and winter, sounding like the scream of a hawk sailing over some farmer's yard, informing me that many restless city merchants are arriving within the circle of the town, or adventurous country traders from the other side. As they come under one horizon, they shout their warning to get off the track to the other, heard sometimes through the circles of two towns.

WALDEN, Chapter IV.

❊ Once when Joe had called again, and we were listening for moose, we heard, come faintly echoing, or creeping from far through the moss-clad aisles, a dull, dry, rushing sound with a solid core to it, yet as if half smothered under the grasp of the luxuriant and fungus-like forest, like the shutting of a door in some distant entry of the damp and shaggy wilderness. If we had not been there, no mortal had heard it. When we asked Joe in a whisper what it was, he answered, "Tree fall!"

THE MAINE WOODS, Chesuncook.

❊ The other evening I was determined I would silence this shallow din; that I would walk in various directions and see if there was not to be found any depth of silence around. As Bonaparte sent out his horsemen in the Red Sea on all sides to find shallow water, so I sent forth my mounted thoughts to find deep water. I left the village and paddled up the river to Fair Haven Pond. As the sun went down, I saw a solitary boatman disporting on the smooth lake. The falling dews seemed to strain and purify

121

the air, and I was smoothed with an infinite stillness. I got the world, as it were, by the nape of the neck, and held it under in the tide of its own events, till it was drowned, and then I let it go downstream like a dead dog. Vast hollow chambers of silence stretched away on every side, and my being expanded in proportion, and filled them. Then first could I appreciate sound, and find it musical.

LETTER TO HARRISON BLAKE, August 8, 1854.

I have been breaking silence these twenty-three years and have hardly made a rent in it.

JOURNAL, February 9, 1841.

As I walk the railroad causeway I am, as the last two months, disturbed by the sound of my steps on the frozen ground. I wish to hear the silence of the night, for the silence is something positive and to be heard. I cannot walk with my ears covered. I must stand still and listen with open ears, far from the noises of the village, that the night may make its impression on me. A fertile and eloquent silence. Sometimes the silence is merely negative, an arid and barren waste in which I shudder, where no ambrosia grows. I must hear the whispering of a myriad voices. Silence alone is worthy to be heard. Silence is of various depth and fertility, like soil. Now it is a mere Sahara, where men perish of hunger and thirst, now a fertile bottom, or prairie, of the West. As I leave the village, drawing nearer to the woods, I listen from time to time to hear the hounds of Silence baying the Moon—to know if they are on the track of any game. If there's no

ON SOUNDS AND SILENCE

Diana in the night, what is it worth? I hark the goddess Diana. The silence rings; it is musical and thrills me. A night in which the silence was audible. I hear the unspeakable.

JOURNAL, January 21, 1853.

⚶ The man I meet with is not often so instructive as the silence he breaks.

JOURNAL, January 7, 1857.

⚶ I mean always to spend only words enough to purchase silence with; and I have found that this, which is so valuable, though many writers do not prize it, does not cost much, after all.

LETTER TO ELLIOT CABOT, March 8, 1848.

⚶ The longest silence is the most pertinent question most pertinently put. Emphatically silent. The most important question, whose answers concern us more than any, are never put in any other way.

JOURNAL, January 4, 1851.

On Poetry ✳ ✳

✳ The poet cherishes his chagrins and sets his sighs to music.

JOURNAL, June 1, 1853.

✳ Poetry *implies* the whole truth. Philosophy *expresses* a particle of it.

JOURNAL, January 26, 1852.

✳ An old poet comes at last to watch his moods as narrowly as a cat does a mouse.

JOURNAL, August 28, 1851.

✳ A man may walk abroad and no more see the sky than if he walked under a shed. The poet is more in the air than the naturalist, though they may walk side by side. Granted that you are out-of-doors; but what if the outer door *is* open, if the inner door is shut! You must walk sometimes perfectly free, not prying nor inquisitive, not bent upon seeing things. Throw away a whole day for a single expansion, a single inspiration of air.

JOURNAL, August 21, 1851.

✳ One sentence of perennial poetry would make me forget, would atone for, volumes of mere science.

JOURNAL, August 5, 1851.

✳ The wayfarer's tree! How good a name! Who bestowed it? How did it get adopted? The mass of men are very unpoetic, yet that Adam that names things is always a poet.

JOURNAL, July 30, 1853.

✳ There is all the poetry in the world in a name. It is a poem which the mass of men hear and read. What is poetry in the common sense, but a string of such jingling names? I want nothing better than a good word. The name of a thing may easily be more than the thing itself to me.

A YANKEE IN CANADA.

✳ The prosaic man sees things badly, or with the bodily sense; but the poet sees them clad in beauty, with the spiritual sense.

JOURNAL, December 9, 1859.

✳ It is interesting to see how the names of famous men are repeated—even of great poets and philosophers. The poet is not known today even by his neighbors to be more than a common man. He is perchance the butt of many. The proud farmer looks down on and boorishly ignores him, or regards him as a loafer who treads down his grass, but perchance in course of time the poet will have so succeeded that some of the farmer's posterity, though equally boorish with their ancestor, will bear the poet's name. The boor names his boy Homer, and so succumbs unknowingly to the bard's victorious fame.

JOURNAL, May 21, 1851.

✳ Most poems, like the fruits, are sweetest toward the blossom end.

JOURNAL, August 23, 1853.

✳ You might frequently say of a poet away from home that he was as mute as a bird of passage, uttering a mere *chip* from time to time, but follow him to his true habitat, and you shall not know him, he will sing so melodiously.

JOURNAL, March 25, 1858.

✳ When I stand in a library where is all the recorded wit of the world, but none of the recording, a mere accumulated and not truly cumulative treasure; where immortal works stand side by side with anthologies that did not survive their month, and cobweb and mildew have already spread from these to the binding of those; and happily I am reminded of what poetry is—I perceive that Shakespeare and Milton did not foresee into what company they were to fall. Alas! that so soon the work of a true poet should be swept into such a dust-hole!

THE WEEK, Friday.

✳ No man is rich enough to keep a poet in his pay.

JOURNAL, March 20, 1858.

On Man 🖋 🖋

🖋 The way to compare men is to compare their respective ideals. The actual man is too complex to deal with.

JOURNAL, 1845–47.

🖋 What a wedge, what a beetle, what a catapult, is an *earnest* man! What can resist him?

LETTER TO HARRISON BLAKE, May 2, 1848.

🖋 The more we know about the ancients, the more we find that they were like the moderns.

JOURNAL, September 2, 1851.

🖋 Man is not at once born into society—hardly into the world. The world that he is hides for a time the world that he inhabits.

JOURNAL, March 14, 1838.

Whether he sleeps or wakes—whether he runs or walks—whether he uses a microscope or a telescope, or his naked eye—a man never discovers anything, never overtakes anything, or leaves anything behind, but himself.

LETTER TO HARRISON BLAKE, May 20, 1860.

Instead of noblemen, let us have noble villages of men. If it is necessary, omit one bridge over the river, go round a little there, and throw one arch at least over the darker gulf of ignorance which surrounds us.

WALDEN, Chapter III.

Any landscape would be glorious to me, if I were assured that its sky was arched over a single hero.

JOURNAL, September 26, 1851.

Every day or two I strolled to the village to hear some of the gossip which is incessantly going on there, circulating either from mouth to mouth, or from newspaper to newspaper, and which, taken in homeopathic doses, was really as refreshing in its way as the rustle of leaves and the peeping of frogs. As I walked in the woods to see the birds and squirrels, so I walked in the village to see the men and boys; instead of the wind among the pines I heard the carts rattle.

WALDEN, Chapter VIII.

A familiar name cannot make a man less strange to me.

JOURNAL, May 21, 1851.

ON MAN

🖎 I cannot conceive of persons more strange to me than they actually are; not thinking, not believing, not doing as I do; interrupted by me. My only distinction must be that I am the greatest bore they ever had. Not in a single thought agreed; regularly balking one another. But when I get far away, my thoughts return to them. That is the way I *can* visit them.

JOURNAL, November 3, 1858.

🖎 But why should not the New Englander try new adventures, and not lay so much stress on his grain, his potato and grass crop, and his orchards—raise other crops than these? Why concern ourselves so much about our beans for seed, and not be concerned at all about a new generation of men?

WALDEN, Chapter VII.

🖎 Men think that it is essential that the *Nation* have commerce, and export ice, and talk through a telegraph, and ride thirty miles an hour, without a doubt, whether *they* do or not; but whether we should live like baboons or like men, is a little uncertain.

WALDEN, Chapter II.

🖎 When we want culture more than potatoes, and illumination more than sugar-plums, then the great resources of a world are taxed and drawn out, and the result, or staple production, is, not slaves, nor operatives, but men—those rare fruits called heroes, saints, poets, philosophers and redeemers.

LIFE WITHOUT PRINCIPLE.

✍ There are nine hundred and ninety-nine patrons of
virtue to one virtuous man.
CIVIL DISOBEDIENCE.

✍ Most men can keep a horse or keep up a certain
fashionable style of living, but few indeed can keep up
great expectations.
JOURNAL, May 6, 1858.

✍ Some men are excited by the smell of burning powder, but I thought in my dream last night how much
saner to be excited by the smell of new bread.
JOURNAL, September 25, 1851.

✍ I raised last summer a squash which weighed 123½
pounds. If it had fallen on me it would have made as
deep and lasting an impression as most men do. I would
just as lief know what it thinks about God as what most
men think, or are said to think. In such a squash you have
already got the bulk of a man. My man, perchance, when
I have put such a question to him, opes his eyes for a moment, essays in vain to think, like a rusty firelock out of
order, then calls for a plate of that same squash to eat and
goes to sleep, as it is called—and that is no great distance
to go, surely.
JOURNAL, January 26, 1858.

✍ Many seem to be so constituted that they can respect only somebody who is dead or something which is
distant.
JOURNAL, November 28, 1860.

ON MAN

🖋 Myriads of arrow-points lie sleeping in the skin of the revolving earth, while meteors revolve in space. The footprint, the mind-print of the oldest men.

JOURNAL, March 28, 1859.

🖋 Time will soon destroy the works of famous painters and sculptors, but the Indian arrowhead will balk his efforts and Eternity will have to come to his aid. They are not fossil bones, but, as it were, fossil thoughts, forever reminding me of the mind that shaped them. I would fain know that I am treading in the tracks of human game— that I am on the trail of mind—and these little reminders never fail to set me right.

JOURNAL, March 28, 1859.

🖋 Every man proposes fairly, and does not willfully take the devil for his guide; as our shadows never fall between us and the sun. Go toward the sun and your shadow will fall behind you.

JOURNAL, February 8, 1841.

🖋 I think that the existence of man in nature is the divinest and most startling of all facts. It is a fact which few have realized.

JOURNAL, May 21, 1851.

🖋 A robust poor man, one sunny day here in Concord, praised a fellow-townsman to me, because, as he said, he was kind to the poor; meaning himself. The kind uncles and aunts of the race are more esteemed than its true spiritual fathers and mothers.

WALDEN, Chapter I.

He who gives himself entirely to his fellow-men appears to them useless and selfish; but he who gives himself partially to them is pronounced a benefactor and philanthropist.

CIVIL DISOBEDIENCE.

I love to see the herd of men feeding heartily on coarse and succulent pleasures, as cattle on the husks and stalks of vegetables. Though there are many crooked and crabbed specimens of humanity among them, run all to thorn and rind, and crowded out of shape by adverse circumstances, like the third chestnut in the bur, so that you wonder to see some heads wear a whole hat, yet fear not that the race will fail or waver in them; like the crabs which grow in hedges, they furnish the stocks of sweet and thrifty fruits still. Thus is nature recruited from age to age, while the fair and palatable varieties die out, and have their period. This is that mankind. How cheap must be the material of which so many men are made!

THE WEEK, Friday.

Why is it that in the lives of men we hear more of the dark wood than of the sunny pasture?

JOURNAL, October 29, 1857.

The papers are talking about the prospects of a war between England and America. Neither side sees how its country can avoid a long and fratricidal war without sacrificing its honor. Both nations are ready to take a desperate step, to forget the interests of civilization and Christianity and their commercial prosperity and fly at each other's throats. When I see an individual thus beside himself, thus desperate, ready to shoot or be shot, like a blackleg who has little to lose, no serene aims to accomplish, I think he is a candidate for bedlam. What asylum is there for nations to go to? Nations are thus ready to talk of wars and challenge one another, because they are made up to such an extent of poor, low-spirited, despairing men, in whose eyes the chance of shooting somebody else without being shot themselves exceeds their actual good fortune. Who, in fact, will be the first to enlist but the most desperate class, they who have lost all hope? And they may at last infect the rest.

JOURNAL, February 27, 1856.

In order to avoid delusions, I would fain let man go by and behold a universe in which man is but as a grain of sand.

JOURNAL, April 2, 1852.

Though the parents cannot determine whether the child shall be male or female, yet, methinks, it depends on them whether he shall be a worthy addition to the human family.

JOURNAL, November 23, 1852.

Often we are so jarred by chagrins in dealing with the world, that we cannot reflect. Everything beautiful impresses us as sufficient to itself. Many men who have had much intercourse with the world and not borne the trial well affect me as all resistance, all bur and rind, without any gentleman, or tender and innocent core left. They have become hedgehogs.

JOURNAL, October 26, 1853.

🖎 With all this opportunity, this comedy and tragedy, how near all men come to doing nothing! It is strange that they did not make us more intense and emphatic, that they do not goad us into some action. Generally, with all our desires and restlessness, we are no more likely to embark in any enterprise than a tree is to walk to a more favorable locality.

JOURNAL, May 29, 1857.

🖎 When I meet gentlemen and ladies, I am reminded of the extent of the inhabitable and uninhabitable globe; I exclaim to myself, Surfaces! Surfaces! If the outside of a man is so variegated and extensive, what must the inside be?

JOURNAL, March 10, 1859.

🖎 The New-Englander is a pagan suckled in a creed outworn. Superstition has always reigned. It is absurd to think that these farmers, dressed in their Sunday clothes, proceeding to church, differ essentially in this respect from the Roman peasantry. They have merely changed the names and number of their gods. Men were as good then as they are now, and loved one another as much—or little.

JOURNAL, June 4, 1853.

🖎 I find the prophets and preachers employed in excusing the ways of men.

JOURNAL, March 4, 1852.

🖎 How prompt we are to satisfy the hunger and thirst of our bodies; how slow to satisfy the hunger and thirst

of our *souls!* Indeed, we would-be practical folks cannot
use this word without blushing because of our infidelity,
having starved this substance almost to a shadow. We
feel it to be as absurd as if a man were to break forth into
a eulogy on *his dog,* who hasn't any.

LETTER TO HARRISON BLAKE, February 27, 1853.

One sensible act will be more memorable than a
monument as high as the moon.

JOURNAL, June 26, 1852.

I do not think that man can understand the *importance* of man's existence, its bearing on the other
phenomena of life, until it shall become a remembrance
to him the survivor that such a being or such a race once
existed on the earth. Imagine yourself alone in the world,
a musing, wondering, reflecting spirit, *lost* in thought,
and imagine thereafter the creation of man!—man made
in the image of God!

JOURNAL, May 21, 1851.

If you aspire to anything better than politics, expect
no cooperation from men. They will not further anything
good. You must prevail of your own force, as a plant
springs and grows by its own vitality.

JOURNAL, April 3, 1858.

Man has a million eyes, and the race knows infinitely more than the individual. Consent to be wise
through your race.

JOURNAL, September 15, 1850.

🖎 I think that the standing miracle to man is man. Behind the paling yonder, come rain or shine, hope or doubt, there dwells a man, an actual being who can sympathize with our sublimest thoughts.

JOURNAL, May 21, 1851.

On the Seasons 🌿 🌿

🌿 Live in each season as it passes; breathe the air, drink the drink, taste the fruit, and resign yourself to the influences of each.

JOURNAL, August 23, 1853.

🌿 The year has many seasons more than are recognized in the almanac.

JOURNAL, 1850.

🌿 As a child looks forward to the coming of the summer, so could we contemplate with quiet joy the circle of the seasons returning without fail eternally.

JOURNAL, January 6, 1838.

🌿 No one, to my knowledge, has observed the minute differences in the seasons. Hardly two nights are alike.

JOURNAL, June 11, 1851.

❧ Each season is but an infinitesimal point. It no sooner comes than it is gone. It has no duration. It simply gives a tone and hue to my thought. Each annual phenomenon is a reminiscence and prompting. Our thoughts and sentiments answer to the revolutions of the seasons, as two cog-wheels fit into each other. We are conversant with only one point of contact at a time, from which we receive a prompting and impulse and instantly pass to a new season or point of contact. A year is made up of a certain series and number of sensations and thoughts which have their language in nature. Now I am ice, now I am sorrel. Each experience reduces itself to a mood of the mind.

JOURNAL, June 6, 1857.

❧ The seasons do not cease a moment to revolve, and therefore Nature rests no longer at her culminating point than at any other. If you are not out at the right instant, the summer may go by and you not see it. How much of the year is spring and fall, how little can be called summer! The grass is no sooner grown than it begins to wither.

JOURNAL, August 19, 1851.

❧ The year is but a succession of days, and I see that I could assign some office to each day which, summed up, would be the history of the year. Everything is done in season, and there is no time to spare.

JOURNAL, August 24, 1852.

❀ No mortal is alert enough to be present at the first dawn of the spring.

JOURNAL, March 17, 1857.

❀ The sky appears broader now than it did. The day has opened its eyelids wider. The lengthening of the days, commenced a good while ago, is a kind of fore-runner of the spring.

JOURNAL, February 19, 1852.

❀ The first pleasant days of spring come out like a squirrel and go in again.

JOURNAL, March 7, 1855.

❀ One attraction in coming to the woods to live was that I should have leisure and opportunity to see the Spring come in.

WALDEN, Chapter XVII.

❀ Shall not a man have his spring as well as the plants?

JOURNAL, June, 1850.

❀ It seems to take but one summer day to fetch the summer in.

JOURNAL, May 18, 1851.

❀ And so the seasons went rolling on into summer, as one rambles into higher and higher grass.

WALDEN, Chapter XVII.

❀ There is no plateau on which Nature rests at mid-summer, but she instantly commences the descent to winter.

JOURNAL, August 23, 1858.

❧ Do not the flowers of August and September generally resemble suns and stars—sunflowers and asters and the single flowers of the goldenrod?

JOURNAL, August 6, 1853.

❧ The sound of the crickets gradually prevails more and more. I hear the year falling asleep.

JOURNAL, August 20, 1852.

❧ Summer is gone with all its infinite wealth, and still nature is genial to man. Though he no longer bathes in the stream, or reclines on the bank, or plucks berries on the hills, still he beholds the same inaccessible beauty around him.

JOURNAL, November 22, 1860.

❧ October is the month for painted leaves. Their rich glow now flashes round the world. As fruits and leaves and the day itself acquire a bright tint just before they fall, so the year near its setting. October is its sunset sky; November the later twilight.

AUTUMNAL TINTS.

❧ I wonder that the very cows and the dogs in the street do not manifest a recognition of the bright tints about and above them. I saw a terrier dog glance up and down the painted street before he turned in at his master's gate, and I wondered what he thought of those lit trees— if they did not touch his philosophy or spirits—but I fear he had only his common doggish thoughts after all. He trotted down the yard as if it were a matter of course after all, or else as if he deserved it all.

JOURNAL, October 9, 1860.

❀ October answers to that period in the life of man when he is no longer dependent on his transient moods, when all his experience ripens into wisdom, but every root, branch, leaf of him glows with maturity. What he has been and done in his spring and summer appears. He bears his fruit.

JOURNAL, November 14, 1853.

❀ Now the year itself begins to be ripe, ripened by the frost, like a persimmon.

JOURNAL, October 4, 1859.

❀ The cornstalks are stacked like muskets along the fields.

JOURNAL, September 17, 1852.

❀ Brown is the color for me, the color of our coats and our daily lives, the color of the poor man's loaf. The bright tints are pies and cakes, good only for October feasts, which would make us sick if eaten every day.

JOURNAL, March 28, 1859.

❀ The dry grasses are not dead for me. A beautiful form has as much life at one season as another.

JOURNAL, November 11, 1850.

❀ All the light of November may be called an afterglow.

JOURNAL, November 10, 1858.

❧ Nature now, like an athlete, begins to strip herself in earnest for her contest with her great antagonist Winter. In the bare trees and twigs what a display of muscle!

JOURNAL, October 29, 1858.

❧ How pleasant a sense of preparedness for the winter—plenty of wood in the shed and potatoes and apples, etc., in the cellar, and the house banked up! Now it will be a cheerful sight to see the snows descend and hear the blast howl.

JOURNAL, December 13, 1855.

❧ Before I finally went into winter quarters in November, I used to resort to the northeast side of Walden, which the sun, reflected from the pitch pine woods and the stony shore, made the fireside of the pond; it is so much pleasanter and wholesomer to be warmed by the sun while you can be, than by an artificial fire. I thus warmed myself by the still glowing embers which the summer, like a departed hunter, had left.

WALDEN, Chapter XIII.

❧ If the race had never lived through a winter, what would they think was coming?

JOURNAL, November 8, 1850.

❧ Now all that moves migrates, or has migrated. Ducks have gone by. The citizen has sought the town.

JOURNAL, November 14, 1858.

ON THE SEASONS

✿ Why do you flee so soon, sir, to the theaters, lecture-rooms, and museums of the city? If you will stay here awhile I will promise you strange sights. You shall walk on water; all these brooks and rivers and ponds shall be your highway. You shall see the whole earth covered a foot or more deep with purest white crystals, in which you slump or over which you glide, and all the trees and stubble glittering in icy armor.

JOURNAL, October 18, 1859.

✿ The animal merely makes him a bed, which he warms with his body in a sheltered place. He does not make a house. But man, having discovered fire, warms a spacious apartment up to the same temperature with his body, and without robbing it, so that he can divest himself of cumbersome clothing—not keeping his bed—maintain a kind of summer in the midst of winter, and, by means of windows, even admit the light. It was his invention to box up some air and warm it, make that his bed, and in this live and move and have his being still, and breathe as in a congenial climate or summer, without taking to his bed. Thus he goes a step or two beyond instinct and secures a little time for the fine arts.

JOURNAL, February 5, 1854.

✿ Though winter is represented in the almanac as an old man, facing the wind and sleet, and drawing his cloak about him, we rather think of him as a merry wood-chopper, and warm-blooded youth, as blithe as summer.

A WINTER WALK.

143

❁ In winter we lead a more inward life. Our hearts are warm and cheery, like cottages under drifts, whose windows and doors are half concealed, but from whose chimneys the smoke cheerfully ascends. The imprisoning drifts increase the sense of comfort which the house affords, and in the coldest days we are content to sit over the hearth and see the sky through the chimney-top, enjoying the quiet and serene life that may be had in a warm corner by the chimneyside, or feeling our pulse by listening to the low of cattle in the street, or the sound of the flail in distant barns all the long afternoon. No doubt a skillful physician could determine our health by observing how these simple and natural sounds affected us.

A WINTER WALK.

❁ To the healthy man the winter of his discontent never comes.

JOURNAL, October 13, 1851.

❁ Now, by 2 P.M., a regular snowstorm has commenced, fine flakes falling steadily, and rapidly whitening all the landscape. In half an hour the russet earth is painted white even to the horizon. Do we know of any other so silent and sudden a change?

JOURNAL, November 28, 1858.

❁ Never is there so much light in the air as in one of these bright winter afternoons, when all the earth is covered with new-fallen snow and there is not a cloud in the sky. The sky is much the darkest side, like the bluish lining of an egg-shell. There seems nothing left to make night out of. With this white earth beneath and that spotless skimmed-milk sky above him, man is but a black speck inclosed in a white egg-shell.

JOURNAL, February 13, 1859.

🏵 How completely a load of hay in the winter revives the memory of past summers! Summer in us is only a little dried like it.

JOURNAL, January 5, 1858.

🏵 What a world we live in! Where myriads of these little disks, so beautiful to the most prying eye, are whirled down on every traveler's coat, the observant and the unobservant, and on the restless squirrel's fur, and on the far-stretching fields and forests, the wooded dells, and the mountain-tops. Far, far away from the haunts of man, they roll down some little slope, fall over and come to their bearings, and melt or lose their identity in the mass, ready anon to swell some little rill with their contribution, and so, at last, the universal ocean from which they came. There they lie, like the wreck of chariot-wheels after a battle in the skies. Meanwhile the meadow mouse shoves them aside in his gallery, the schoolboy casts them in his snowball, or the woodsman's sled glides smoothly over them, these glorious spangles, the sweeping of heaven's floor. And they all sing, melting as they sing of the mysteries of the number six—six, six, six. He takes up the water of the sea in his hand, leaving the salt; He disperses it in mist through the skies; He recollects and sprinkles it like grain in six-rayed snowy stars over the earth, there to lie till He dissolves its bonds again.

JOURNAL, January 5, 1856.

❀ The winter, with its snow and ice, is not an evil to be corrected. It is as it was designed and made to be, for the artist has had leisure to add beauty to use.

JOURNAL, December 11, 1855.

❀ Is not January alone pure winter? December belongs to the fall; it is a wintery November: February to the spring; it is a snowy March.

JOURNAL, February 9, 1854.

❀ If in the winter there are fewer men in the fields and woods—and in the *country* generally—you see the tracks of those who had preceded you, and so are more reminded of them than in summer.

JOURNAL, December 12, 1859.

❀ In winter, nature is a cabinet of curiosities, full of dried specimens, in their natural order and position. The meadows and forests are a *hortus siccus.* The leaves and grasses stand perfectly pressed by the air without screw or gum, and the birds' nests are not hung on an artificial twig, but where they builded them.

A WINTER WALK.

❀ We love to think in winter, as we walk over the snowy pastures, of those happy dreamers that lie under the sod, of dormice and all that race of dormant creatures, which have such a superfluity of life enveloped in thick folds of fur, impervious to cold.

THE WEEK, Sunday.

❀ The coldest night for a long, long time was last. Sheets froze stiff about the faces. Cat mewed to have the door opened, but was at first disinclined to go out. When she came in at nine she smelt of meadow-hay. We all took her up and smelled of her, it was so fragrant. Had cuddled in some barn. People dreaded to go to bed. The ground cracked in the night as if a powder-mill had blown up, and the timbers of the house also. My pail of water was frozen in the morning so that I could not break it. Must leave many buttons unbuttoned, owing to numb fingers. Iron was like fire in the hands. Thermometer at about 7:30 A.M. gone into the bulb, —19° at least. The cold has stopped the clock. Every bearded man in the street is a gray-beard. Bread, milk, meat, cheese, etc., etc., all frozen. See the inside of your cellar door all covered and sparkling with frost like Golconda. Pity the poor who have not a large woodpile. The latches are white with frost, and every nailhead in entries, etc., has a white cap. The chopper hesitates to go to the woods.

JOURNAL, February 7, 1855.

❀ Is not January the hardest month to get through? When you have weathered that, you get into the gulf-stream of winter, nearer the shores of spring.

JOURNAL, February 2, 1854.

❀ After the January thaw our thoughts cease to refer to autumn and we look forward to spring.

JOURNAL, January 9, 1860.

147

❀ To us snow and cold seem a mere delaying of the spring. How far we are from understanding the value of these things in the economy of Nature!

JOURNAL, March 8, 1859.

❀ In winter, after middle, we are interested in what is springlike.

JOURNAL, January 25, 1853.

❀ We are hunters pursuing the summer on snowshoes and skates, all winter long. There is really but one season in our hearts.

JOURNAL, December 6, 1856.

On the Art of Writing 🖋 🖋

🖋 Whatever book or sentence will bear to be read twice, we may be sure was thought twice.

JOURNAL, March 18, 1842.

🖋 The forcible writer stands bodily behind his words with his experience. He does not make books out of books, but he has been *there* in person.

JOURNAL, February 3, 1852.

🖋 Nothing goes by luck in composition. It allows of no tricks. The best you can write will be the best you are. Every sentence is the result of a long probation. The author's character is read from title-page to end. Of this he never corrects the proofs.

JOURNAL, February 28, 1841.

🖋 Though I write every day, yet when I say a good thing it seems as if I wrote but rarely.

JOURNAL, February 26, 1841.

There are two classes of authors: the one write the history of their times, the other their biography.

JOURNAL, April 20, 1841.

If thou art a writer, write as if thy time were short, for it is indeed short at the longest.

JOURNAL, January 24, 1852.

Time never passes so quickly and unaccountably as when I am engaged in composition, i.e. in writing down my thoughts. Clocks seem to have been put forward.

JOURNAL, January 27, 1858.

It is not easy to write in a journal what interests us at any time, because to write is not what interests us.

THE WEEK, Thursday.

It is a great art in the writer to improve from day to day just that soil and fertility which he has, to harvest that crop which his life yields, whatever it may be, not be straining as if to reach apples or oranges when he yields only ground-nuts. He should be digging, not soaring. Just as earnest as your life is, so deep is your soil. If strong and deep, you will sow wheat and raise bread of life in it.

JOURNAL, November 9, 1858.

It is wise to write on many subjects, to try many themes, that so you may find the right and inspiring one. You must try a thousand themes before you find the right one, as nature makes a thousand acorns to get one oak.

JOURNAL, September 4, 1851.

Letter-writing too often degenerates into a communicating of facts, and not truths.

LETTER TO HELEN THOREAU, October 27, 1837.

In writing, conversation should be folded many times thick. It is the height of art that, on the first perusal, plain common sense should appear; on the second, severe truth; and on a third, beauty; and, having these warrants for its depth and reality, we may then enjoy the beauty for evermore.

LETTER TO RALPH W. EMERSON, July 8, 1843.

No man's thoughts are new, but the style of their expression is the never-failing novelty which cheers and refreshes men.

THOMAS CARLYLE.

What if there were a tariff on words, on language, for the encouragement of home manufactures? Have we not the genius to coin our own? Let the schoolmaster distinguish the true from the counterfeit.

JOURNAL, October 16, 1859.

How many there are who advise you to print! How few who advise you to lead a more interior life! In the one case there is all the world to advise you, in the other there is none to advise you but yourself. Nobody ever advised me not to print but myself. The public persuade the author to print, as the meadow invites the brook to fall into it.

JOURNAL, April 16, 1852.

🐝 I wish I could buy at the shops some kind of india-rubber that would rub out at once all that in my writing which it now costs me so many perusals, so many months if not years, and so much reluctance, to erase.

JOURNAL, *December 27, 1853.*

🐝 I find incessant labor with the hands, which engrosses the attention also, the best method to remove palaver out of one's style.

JOURNAL, *January 5, 1842.*

🐝 It is vain to try to write unless you feel strong in the knees.

JOURNAL, *August 9, 1841.*

🐝 He will not idly dance at his work who has wood to cut and cord before nightfall in the short days of winter; but every stroke will be husbanded, and ring soberly through the wood; and so will the strokes of that scholar's pen, which at evening record the story of the day, ring soberly, yet cheerily, on the ear of the reader, long after the echoes of his axe have died away. The scholar may be sure that he writes the tougher truth for the calluses on his palms. They give firmness to the sentence. Indeed, the mind never makes a great and successful effort, without a corresponding energy of the body. We are often struck by the force and precision of style to which hard-working men, unpracticed in writing, easily attain when required to make the effort. As if plainness and vigor and sincerity, the ornaments of style, were better learned on the farm and in the workshop than in the schools. The sentences written by such rude hands are nervous and tough, like hardened thongs, the sinews of the deer, or the roots of the pine.

THE WEEK, Sunday.

When we consider the weak and nerveless periods of some literary men, who perchance in feet and inches come up to the standard of their race, and are not deficient in girth also, we are amazed at the immense sacrifice of thews and sinews. What! these proportions, these bones—and this their work! Hands that could have felled an ox have hewed this fragile matter which would not have tasked a lady's fingers!

THE WEEK, Sunday.

Language is the most perfect work of art in the world. The chisel of a thousand years retouches it.

JOURNAL, July 27, 1840.

Who cares what a man's style is, so it is intelligible— as intelligible as his thought. Literally and really, the style is no more than the *stylus,* the pen he writes with; and it is not worth scraping and polishing, and gilding, unless it will write his thoughts the better for it. It is something for use, and not to look at. The question for us is not whether Pope had a fine style, wrote with a peacock's feather, but whether he uttered useful thoughts. Translate a book a dozen times from one language to another, and what becomes of its style? Most books would be worn out and disappear in this ordeal. The pen which wrote it is soon destroyed, but the poem survives.

THOMAS CARLYLE.

✠ As for style of writing, if one has anything to say, it drops from him simply and directly as a stone falls to the ground. There are no two ways about it, but down it comes, and he may stick in the points and stops wherever he can get a chance. New ideas come into this world somewhat like falling meteors, with a flash and an explosion, and perhaps somebody's castle-roof perforated. To try to polish the stone in its descent, to give it a peculiar turn, and make it whistle a tune, perchance, would be of no use, if it were possible. Your polished stuff turns out not to be meteoric, but of this earth.

LETTER TO DANIEL RICKETSON, August 18, 1857.

✠ A well-built sentence, in the rapidity and force with which it works, may be compared to a modern corn-planter, which furrows out, drops the seed, and covers it up at one movement.

JOURNAL, January 5, 1842.

✠ The writer must direct his sentences as carefully and leisurely as the marksman his rifle, who shoots sitting and with a rest, with patent sights and conical balls beside. He must not merely seem to speak the truth. He must really speak it. If you foresee that a part of your essay will topple down after the lapse of time, throw it down now yourself.

JOURNAL, January 26, 1852.

✠ Men should not go to New Zealand to write or think of Greece and Rome, nor more to New England. New earths, new themes expect us. Celebrate not the Garden of Eden, but your own.

JOURNAL, October 22, 1857.

154

He who gives us only the results of other men's lives, though with brilliant temporary success, we may in some measure justly accuse of having defrauded us of our time. We want him to give us that which was most precious to him—not his life's blood but even that for which his life's blood circulated, what he got by living. If anything ever yielded him pure pleasure or instruction, let him communicate it. Let the money-getter tell us how much he loves wealth, and what means he takes to accumulate it. He must describe those facts which he knows and loves better than anybody else. He must not write on foreign missions.

JOURNAL, 1837–47.

Write while the heat is in you. When the farmer burns a hole in his yoke, he carries the hot iron quickly from the fire to the wood, for every moment it is less effectual to penetrate it. It must be used instantly, or it is useless. The writer who postpones the recording of his thoughts uses an iron which has cooled to burn a hole with. He cannot inflame the minds of his audience.

JOURNAL, February 10, 1852.

Nature never indulges in exclamations, never says Ah! or Alas! She is not of French descent. She is a plain writer, uses few gestures, does not add to her verbs, uses few adverbs, uses no expletives. I find that I use many words for the sake of emphasis which really add nothing to the force of my sentences, and they look relieved the

155

moment I have cancelled these. Words by which I express my mood, my conviction, rather than the simple truth.

JOURNAL, January 26, 1852.

The words of some men are thrown forcibly against you and adhere like burs.

JOURNAL, June 4, 1839.

How vain it is to sit down to write when you have not stood up to live!

JOURNAL, August 19, 1851.

I am thinking by what long discipline and at what cost a man learns to speak simply at last.

JOURNAL, December 12, 1851.

It is enough if I have pleased myself with writing; I am then sure of an audience.

JOURNAL, March 24, 1842.

I esteem it a rare happiness to be able to *write* anything, but there (if I ever get there) my concern for it is apt to end. Time & Co. are, after all, the only quite honest and trustworthy publishers that we know. I can sympathize, perhaps, with the barberry bush, whose business it is solely to *ripen* its fruit (though that may not be to sweeten it) and to protect it with thorns, so that it holds on all winter, even, unless some hungry crows come to pluck it.

LETTER TO ELLIOT CABOT, March 8, 1848.

Many a man who should rather describe his dinner imposes on us with a history of the Grand Khan.

JOURNAL, November 18, 1857.

We like to read a good description of no thing so well as that which we already know the best, as our friend, or ourselves even.

JOURNAL, October 13, 1860.

We sometimes experience a mere fullness of life, which does not find any channel to flow into. We are stimulated, but to no obvious purpose. I feel myself uncommonly prepared for *some* literary work, but I can select no work. I am prepared not so much for contemplation, as for forceful expression. I am braced both physically and intellectually. It is not so much the music as the marching to the music that I feel.

JOURNAL, September 7, 1851.

The grammarian is often one who can neither cry nor laugh, yet thinks that he can express human emotions. So the posture-masters tell you how you shall walk— turning your toes out, perhaps, excessively—but so the beautiful walkers are not made.

JOURNAL, January 2, 1859.

My work is writing, and I do not hesitate, though I know that no subject is too trivial for me, tried by ordinary standards; for, ye fools, the theme is nothing, the life is everything. All that interests the reader is the depth and intensity of the life excited. We touch our subject but by a point which has no breadth, but the pyramid of our experience, or our interest in it, rests on us by a broader or narrower base.

JOURNAL, October 18, 1856.

From the weak and flimsy periods of the politician and literary man, we are glad to turn even to the description of work, the simple record of the month's labor in the farmer's almanac, to restore our tone and spirits. A sentence should read as if its author, had he held a plow instead of a pen, could have drawn a furrow deep and straight to the end.

THE WEEK, Sunday.

If you indulge in long periods, you must be sure to have a snapper at the end.

LETTER TO DANIEL RICKETSON, August 18, 1857.

It is fatal to the writer to be too much possessed by his thought. Things must lie a little remote to be described.

JOURNAL, November 11, 1851.

Shall I not have words as fresh as my thoughts? Shall I use any other man's word? A genuine thought or feeling can find expression for itself, if it have to invent hieroglyphics. It has the universe for type-metal. It is for want of original thought that one man's style is like another's.

JOURNAL, September 8, 1851.

Improve every opportunity to express yourself in writing, as if it were your last.

JOURNAL, December 17, 1851.

In books, that which is most generally interesting is what comes home to the most cherished private experience of the greatest number. It is not the book of him who has traveled the farthest over the surface of the globe, but of him who has lived the deepest and been the most at home.

JOURNAL, November 20, 1857.

Thinkers and writers are in foolish haste to come before the world with crude works. Young men are persuaded by their friends, or by their own restless ambition, to write a course of lectures in a summer against the ensuing winter; and what it took the lecturer a summer to write, it will take his audience but an hour to forget. If time is short, then you have no time to waste.

JOURNAL, November 16, 1851.

On Experience ❀ ❀

❀ Who is old enough to have learned from experience?
JOURNAL, March 21, 1842.

❀ The value of any experience is measured, of course, not by the amount of money, but the amount of development we get out of it.
JOURNAL, November 26, 1860.

❀ Early for several mornings I have heard the sound of a flail. It leads me to ask if I have spent as industrious a spring and summer as the farmer, and gathered as rich a crop of experience. If so, the sound of my flail will be heard by those who have ears to hear, separating the kernel from the chaff all the fall and winter, and a sound no less cheering it will be.
JOURNAL, August 29, 1854.

ON EXPERIENCE

✻ There is no such thing as pure *objective* observation. Your observation, to be interesting, i.e. to be significant, must be *subjective*. The sum of what the writer of whatever class has to report is simply some human experience, whether he be poet or philosopher or man of science. The man of most science is the man most alive, whose life is the greatest event. Senses that take cognizance of outward things merely are of no avail. It matters not where or how far you travel—the farther commonly the worse—but how much alive you are. If it is possible to conceive of an event outside to humanity, it is not of the slightest significance, though it were the explosion of a planet. Every important worker will report what life there is in him. It makes no odds into what seeming deserts the poet is born. Though all his neighbors pronounce it a Sahara, it will be a paradise to him; for the desert which we see is the result of the barrenness of our experience.

JOURNAL, May 6, 1854.

✻ In the summer we lay up a stock of experiences for the winter, as the squirrel of nuts—something for conversation in winter evenings.

JOURNAL, September 4, 1851.

✻ Surely one may as profitably be soaked in the juices of a swamp for one day as pick his way dry-shod over sand. Cold and damp—are they not as rich experience as warmth and dryness?

THE WEEK, Thursday.

❁ Our life is not altogether a forgetting, but also, alas, to a great extent a remembering, of that which perchance we should never have been conscious of—the consciousness of what should not be permitted to disturb a man's waking hours.

JOURNAL, November 10, 1851.

❁ When a generation or two have used up all the enemies' darts, their successors lead a comparatively easy life. We owe to our fathers analogous blessings. Many old people receive pensions for no other reason, it seems to me, but as a compensation for having lived a long time ago. No doubt our town dogs still talk, in a snuffling way, about the days that tried dogs' noses.

THE MAINE WOODS, Chesuncook.

❁ I think that no experience which I have today comes up to, or is comparable with, the experiences of my boyhood.

JOURNAL, July 16, 1851.

❁ Whole weeks and months of my summer life slide away in thin volumes like mist and smoke, till at length, some warm morning, perchance, I see a sheet of mist blown down the brook to the swamp, and I float as high above the fields with it. I can recall to mind the stillest summer hours, in which the grasshopper sings over the mulleins, and there is a valor in that time the bare memory of which is armor that can laugh at any blow of fortune.

THE WEEK, Wednesday.

ON EXPERIENCE

✼ A man fits out a ship at great expense and sends it to the West Indies with a crew of men and boys, and after six months or a year it comes back with a load of pineapples. Now if no more gets accomplished than the speculator commonly aims at—if it simply turns out what is called a successful venture—I am less interested in this expedition than in some child's first excursion a-huckle-berrying, in which it is introduced into a new world, experiences a new development, though it brings home only a gill of huckleberries in its basket.

                                                    JOURNAL, November 26, 1860.

On Health and Foods ✖ ✖

✖ 'T is healthy to be sick sometimes.

JOURNAL, 1851.

✖ A man may esteem himself happy when that which is his food is also his medicine.

THE WEEK, Wednesday.

✖ Sickness should not be allowed to extend further than the body. We need only to retreat further within us to preserve uninterrupted the continuity of serene hours to the end of our lives.

JOURNAL, February 14, 1841.

✖ Cultivate the habit of early rising. It is unwise to keep the head long on a level with the feet.

JOURNAL, June 8, 1850.

It is a very remarkable and significant fact that, though no man is quite well or healthy, yet every one believes practically that health is the rule and disease the exception, and each invalid is wont to think of himself in a minority.

JOURNAL, September 3, 1851.

Man begins quarreling with the animal within him, and the result is immediate disease.

JOURNAL, September 3, 1851.

I have noticed that notional nervous invalids, who report to the community the exact condition of their heads and stomachs every morning, as if they alone were blessed or cursed with these parts; who are old betties and quiddies, if men; who can't eat their breakfasts when they are ready, but play with their spoons, and hanker after ice-cream at irregular hours; who go more than half-way to meet any invalidity, and go to bed to be sick on the slightest occasion, in the middle of the brightest forenoon —improve the least opportunity to be sick—I observe that such are self-indulgent persons, without any regular and absorbing employment.

JOURNAL, May 26, 1857.

No doubt the healthiest man in the world is prevented from doing what he would like by sickness.

JOURNAL, December 21, 1855.

Is it not a reproach that man is a carnivorous animal? True, he can and does live, in a great measure, by preying on other animals; but this is a miserable way—as any one who will go to snaring rabbits, or slaughtering lambs, may

165

learn—and he will be regarded as a benefactor of his race who shall teach man to confine himself to a more innocent and wholesome diet.

WALDEN, Chapter XI.

One farmer says to me, "You cannot live on vegetable food solely, for it furnishes nothing to make bones with;" and so he religiously devotes a part of his day to supplying his system with the raw material of bones; walking all the while he talks behind his oxen, which, with vegetable-made bones, jerk him and his lumbering plow along in spite of every obstacle.

WALDEN, Chapter I.

Drink the wines, not of your bottling, but Nature's bottling; not kept in goat-skins or pig-skins, but the skins of a myriad fair berries. Let Nature do your bottling and your pickling and preserving. For all Nature is doing her best each moment to make us well.

JOURNAL, August 23, 1853.

Our appetites have commonly confined our views of ripeness and its phenomena—color and mellowness and perfectness—to the fruits which we eat, and we are wont to forget that an immense harvest which we do not eat, hardly use at all, is annually ripened by nature.

JOURNAL, October 24, 1858.

It is a common saying among country people that if you eat much fried hasty pudding it will make your hair curl. My experience, which was considerable, did not confirm this assertion.

JOURNAL, November 20, 1850.

⚕ The bitter-sweet of a white oak acorn which you nibble in a bleak November walk over the tawny earth is more to me than a slice of imported pineapple. We do not think much of table-fruits. They are especially for aldermen and epicures. They do not feed the imagination. That would starve on them. These wild fruits, whether eaten or not, are a dessert for the imagination. The south may keep her pineapples, and we will be content with our strawberries.

JOURNAL, November 24, 1860.

⚕ As with cold and heat, so with sweet and sour. This natural raciness, sours and bitters etc., which the diseased palate refuses, are the true casters and condiments. What is sour in the house a bracing walk makes sweet. Let your condiments be in the condition of your senses. Apples which the farmer neglects and leaves out as unsalable and unpalatable to those who frequent the markets are choicest fruit to the walker.

JOURNAL, October 29, 1855.

⚕ The invalid, brought to the brink of the grave by an unnatural life, instead of imbibing only the great influence that Nature is, drinks only the tea made of a particular herb, while he still continues his unnatural life—saves at the spile and wastes at the bung. He does not love Nature or his life, and so sickens and dies, and no doctor can cure him.

JOURNAL, August 23, 1853.

⚹ The poor and sick man keeps a horse, often a hostler; but the well man is a horse himself, is horsed on himself; he feels his own oats. First a sound and healthy life, and then spirits to live it with.

JOURNAL, August 10, 1857.

⚹ Measure your health by your sympathy with morning and spring. If there is no response in you to the awakening of nature—if the prospect of an early morning walk does not banish sleep, if the warble of the first bluebird does not thrill you—know that the morning and spring of your life are past. Thus you may feel your pulse.

JOURNAL, February 25, 1859.

⚹ I had yesterday a kink in my back and a general cold, and as usual it amounted to a cessation of life. I lost for a time my *rapport* or relation to nature. Sympathy with nature is an evidence of perfect health.

JOURNAL, November 18, 1857.

⚹ Men have discovered—or think they have discovered —the salutariness of a few wild things only, and not of all nature. Why, "nature" is but another name for health, and the seasons are but different states of health. Some men think that they are not well in the spring, or summer, or autumn, or winter; it is only because they are not *well in* them.

JOURNAL, August 23, 1853.

✄ If you look over a list of medicinal recipes in vogue in the last century, how foolish and useless they are seen to be! And yet we use equally absurd ones with faith today.

JOURNAL, February 18, 1860.

✄ Indeed, I have been sick so long that I have almost forgotten what it is to be well; and yet I feel that it is in all respects only my envelope.

LETTER TO DANIEL RICKETSON, August 15, 1861.

✄ There is consolation in the fact that a particular evil, which perhaps we suffer, is of a venerable antiquity, for it proves its necessity and that it is part of the *order*, not disorder, of the universe. When I realize that the mortality of suckers in the spring is as old a phenomenon, perchance, as the race of suckers itself, I contemplate it with serenity and joy even, as one of the signs of spring. Thus they have fallen on fate. And so, many a fisherman is not seen on the shore who the last spring did not fail here.

JOURNAL, March 28, 1857.

✄ Disease is not the accident of the individual nor even of the generation, but of life itself. In some form, and to some degree or other, it is one of the permanent conditions of life.

JOURNAL, September 3, 1851.

On Trees * *

✳ Nothing stands up more free from blame in this world than a pine tree.

JOURNAL, December 20, 1851.

✳ The fruit of a tree is neither in the seed nor the timber—the full-grown tree—but it is simply the highest use to which it can be put.

JOURNAL, March 7, 1859.

✳ Ah, willow! willow! Would that I always possessed thy good spirits.

JOURNAL, March 18, 1861.

✳ This winter they are cutting down our woods more seriously than ever. Thank God, they cannot cut down the clouds!

JOURNAL, January 21, 1852.

❈ If a man walk in the woods for love of them half of each day, he is in danger of being regarded as a loafer; but if he spends his whole day as a speculator, shearing off those woods and making earth bald before her time, he is esteemed an industrious and enterprising citizen. As if a town had no interest in its forests but to cut them down!

LIFE WITHOUT PRINCIPLE.

❈ It concerns us all whether these proprietors choose to cut down all the woods this winter or not.

JOURNAL, January 22, 1852.

❈ Every larger tree which I knew and admired is being gradually culled out and carried to mill. I miss them as surely and with the same feeling that I do the old inhabitants out of the village street. To me they were something more than timber; to their owners not so.

JOURNAL, December 3, 1855.

❈ These woods! Why do I not feel their being cut more sorely? Does it not affect me nearly? The axe can deprive me of much. Concord is sheared of its pride. I am certainly the less attached to my native town in consequence. One, and a main, link is broken. I shall go to Walden less frequently.

JOURNAL, January 24, 1852.

❈ I do not know but a pine wood is as substantial and as memorable a fact as a friend. I am more sure to come away from it cheered, than from those who come nearest to being my friends.

JOURNAL, December 17, 1851.

⁂ Think how stood the white pine tree on the shore of Chesuncook, its boughs soughing with the four winds, and every individual needle trembling in the sunlight—think how it stands with it now—sold, perchance, to the New England Friction-Match Company!

THE MAINE WOODS, Ktaadn.

⁂ The sugar maple is remarkable for its clean ankle. The groves of these trees looked like vast forest sheds, their branches stopping short at a uniform height, four or five feet from the ground, like eaves, as if they had been trimmed by art, so that you could look under and through the whole grove with its leafy canopy, as under a tent whose curtain is raised.

A YANKEE IN CANADA.

⁂ Well may the tender buds attract us at this season, no less than partridges, for they are the hope of the year, the spring rolled up. The summer is all packed in them.

JOURNAL, January 12, 1855.

⁂ It is remarkable how many beech and chestnut oak leaves, which so recently expanded, have already attained their full size! How they launch themselves forth to the light! How suddenly Nature spreads her umbrellas! How little delay in expanding leaves! They seem to expand before our eyes, like the wings of moths just fallen from the cocoon.

JOURNAL, May 30, 1857.

⁂ The scarlet oak leaf! What a graceful and pleasing outline, a combination of graceful curves and angles! These deep bays in the leaf are agreeable to us as the thought of deep and smooth and secure havens to the mariner. But both your love of repose and your spirit of adventure are addressed, for both bays and headlands are represented—sharp-pointed rocky capes and rounded bays with smooth strands. It is a shore to the aerial ocean, on which the windy surf beats.

JOURNAL, November 11, 1858.

❉ I should not be ashamed to have a shrub oak for my coat-of-arms.

JOURNAL, January 7, 1857.

❉ The odoriferous sassafras, with its delicate green stem, its three-lobed leaf, tempting the traveler to bruise it, it sheds so rare a perfume on him, equal to all the spices of the East. Then its rare-tasting root bark, like nothing else, which I used to dig. The first navigators freighted their ships with it and deemed it worth its weight in gold.

JOURNAL, August 31, 1850.

❉ Many times I thought that if the particular tree, commonly an elm, under which I was walking or riding were the only one like it in the country, it would be worth a journey across the continent to see it. Indeed, I have no doubt that such journeys would be undertaken on hearing a true account of it. But, instead of being confined to a single tree, this wonder was as cheap and common as the air itself. Every man's woodlot was a miracle and surprise to him, and for those who could not go so far there were the trees in the street and the weeds in the yard.

JOURNAL, January 18, 1859.

❋ In the twilight, when you can see only the outlines of the trees in the horizon, the elm-tops indicate where the houses are.

JOURNAL, September, 1950.

❋ There was reason enough for the first settler's selecting the elm out of all the trees of the forest with which to ornament his villages. It is beautiful alike by sunlight and moonlight, and the most beautiful specimens are not the largest. I have seen some only twenty-five or thirty years old, more graceful and healthy, I think, than any others. It is almost become a villageous tree—like martins and bluebirds.

JOURNAL, 1850.

❋ Many large trees, especially elms, about a house are a surer indication of old family distinction and worth than any evidences of wealth. Any evidence of care bestowed on these trees secures the traveler's respect as for a nobler husbandry than the raising of corn and potatoes.

JOURNAL, July 2, 1851.

❋ I have seen many a collection of stately elms which better deserved to be represented at the General Court than the manikins beneath—than the barroom and victualling cellar and groceries they overshadowed. When I see their magnificent domes, miles away in the horizon, over intervening valleys and forests, they suggest a village, a community, there. But, after all, it is a secondary consideration whether there are human dwellings beneath them; these may have long since passed away. I find that into my idea of the village has entered more of the elm than of the human being. They are worth many a political borough. They constitute a borough. The poor human representative of his party sent out from beneath their shade will not suggest a tithe of the dignity, the true nobleness and comprehensiveness of view, the sturdiness and independence, and the serene beneficence that they do.

JOURNAL, January 24, 1856.

�֍ See how artfully the seed of a cherry is placed in order that a bird may be compelled to transport it. It is placed in the very midst of a tempting pericarp, so that the creature that would devour a cherry must take a stone into its mouth. The bird is bribed with the pericarp to take the stone with it and do this little service for Nature. Thus a bird's wing is added to the cherry-stone which was wingless, and it does not wait for winds to transport it.

JOURNAL, September 1, 1860.

✖ The cars on our railroad, and all their passengers, roll over the trunks of trees *sleeping* beneath them which were planted years before the first white man settled in New England.

JOURNAL, November 21, 1860.

✖ It is easier far to recover the history of the trees which stood here a century or more ago than it is to recover the history of the men who walked beneath them. How much do we know—how little more can we know— of these two centuries of Concord life?

JOURNAL, October 19, 1860.

175

✳ The farmer sometimes talks of "brushing up," simply as if bare ground looked better than clothed ground, than that which wears its natural vesture—as if the wild hedges, which, perhaps, are more to his children than his whole farm beside, were *dirt*. I know of one who deserves to be called the Tree-hater, and, perhaps, to leave this for a new patronymic to his children. You would think that he had been warned by an oracle that he would be killed by the fall of a tree, and so was resolved to anticipate them.

THE MAINE WOODS, Chesuncook.

✳ It is not in vain, perhaps, that every winter the forest is brought to our doors, shaggy with lichens. Even in so humble a shape as a wood-pile, it contains sermons for us.

JOURNAL, September 25, 1852.

✳ Now, methinks, the autumnal tints are brightest in our streets and in the woods generally. Stand where half a dozen large elms droop over a house. It is as if you stood within a ripe pumpkin rind, and you feel as mellow as if you were the pulp!

JOURNAL, October 6, 1858.

✳ The oaks stand browned and crisped (amid the pines), their bright colors for the most part burnt out, like a loaf that is baked, and suggest an equal wholesomeness. The whole tree is now not only ripe but, as it were, a fruit perfectly cooked by the sun. That same sun which called forth its leaves in the spring has now, aided by the frost, sealed up their fountains for the year and withered

176

them. The order has gone forth for them to rest. As each tree casts its leaves it stands careless and free, like a horse freed from his harness, or like one who has done his year's work and now stands unnoticed, but with concentrated strength and contentment, ready to brave the blasts of winter without a murmur.

JOURNAL, October 22, 1858.

✳ But no weather interfered fatally with my walks, or rather my going abroad, for I frequently tramped eight or ten miles through the deepest snow to keep an appointment with a beech tree, or a yellow birch, or an old acquaintance among the pines.

WALDEN, Chapter XIV.

✳ Is it the lumberman, then, who is the friend and lover of the pine, stands nearest to it, and understands its nature best? Is it the tanner who has barked it, or he who has boxed it for turpentine, whom posterity will fable to have been changed into a pine at last? No, No! it is the poet; he it is who makes the truest use of the pine, who does not fondle it with an axe, nor tickle it with a saw, nor stroke it with a plane, who knows whether its heart is false without cutting into it, who has not bought the stumpage of the township on which it stands. All the pines shudder and heave a sigh when *that* man steps on the forest floor. No, it is the poet, who loves them as his own shadow in the air, and lets them stand. I have been into the lumber-yard, and the carpenter's shop, and the tannery, and the lampblack factory, and the turpentine clearing; but when at length I saw the tops of the pines waving and reflecting the light at a distance high over all the rest of the forest, I realized that the former were not the highest use of the pine. It is not their bones or hide or tallow that I love most. It is the living spirit of the tree, not its spirit of turpentine, with which I can sympathize, and which heals my cuts. It is as immortal as I am, and perchance will go to as high a heaven, there to tower above me still.

THE MAINE WOODS, Chesuncook.

On Society ✍ ✍

✍ Our employment generally is tinkering, mending the old worn-out teapot of society. Our stock in trade is solder.

JOURNAL, August 30, 1856.

✍ The social condition of genius is the same in all ages. Aeschylus was undoubtedly alone and without sympathy in his simple reverence for the mystery of the universe.

JOURNAL, January 29, 1840.

✍ The society which I was made for is not here.

JOURNAL, July 19, 1851.

✍ I see nothing permanent in the society around me, and am not quite committed to any of its ways.

JOURNAL, 1850.

✍ Society is commonly too cheap. We meet at very short intervals, not having had time to acquire any new value for each other.

WALDEN, Chapter V.

⬔ Individuals, like nations, must have suitable broad and natural boundaries, even a considerable neutral ground, between them.

WALDEN, Chapter VI.

⬔ I am not responsible for the successful working of the machinery of society. I am not the son of the engineer. I perceive that, when an acorn and a chestnut fall side by side, the one does not remain inert to make way for the other, but both obey their own laws, and spring and grow and flourish as best they can, till one, perchance, over-shadows and destroys the other. If a plant cannot live according to its nature, it dies; and so a man.

CIVIL DISOBEDIENCE.

⬔ What men call social virtues, good fellowship, is comonly but the virtue of pigs in a litter, which lie close together to keep each other warm. It brings men together in crowds and mobs in barrooms and elsewhere, but it does not deserve the name of virtue.

JOURNAL, October 23, 1852.

⬔ What a generation this is! It travels with some brains in its hat, with a couple of spare cigars on top of them. It carries its heart in its breast, covered by a lozenge in its waistcoat pocket.

JOURNAL, September, 1850.

⬔ The society of young women is the most unprofitable I have ever tried. They are so light and flighty that you can never be sure whether they are there or not there.

JOURNAL, November 14, 1851.

🖋 Men talk to me about society as if I had none and they had some, as if it were only to be got by going to the sociable or to Boston.

JOURNAL, March 27, 1857.

🖋 Emerson says that his life is so unprofitable and shabby for the most part, that he is driven to all sorts of resources, and, among the rest, to men. I tell him that we differ only in our resources. Mine is to get away from men.

LETTER TO HARRISON BLAKE, August 8, 1854.

🖋 I live in an angle of a leaden wall, into whose composition was poured a little alloy of bell-metal. Often, in the repose of my mid-day, there reaches my ears a confused *tintinnabulum* from without. It is the noise of my contemporaries.

WALDEN, Chapter XVIII.

🖋 There are a thousand hacking at the branches of evil to one who is striking at the root, and it may be that he who bestows the largest amount of time and money on the needy is doing the most by his mode of life to produce that misery which he strives in vain to relieve. It is the pious slave-breeder devoting the proceeds of every tenth slave to buy Sunday liberty for the rest.

WALDEN, Chapter I.

🖋 One afternoon, near the end of the first summer, when I went to the village to get a shoe from the cobbler's, I was seized and put into jail, because, as I have elsewhere related, I did not pay a tax to, or recognize the authority of, the State which buys and sells men, women, and children, like cattle, at the door of its senate-house. I had gone down to the woods for other purposes. But, wherever a man goes, men will pursue and paw him with their dirty institutions, and, if they can, constrain him to belong to their desperate odd-fellow society. It is true, I might have resisted forcibly with more or less effect, might have run "amok" against society; but I preferred that society should run "amok" against me, it being the desperate party.

WALDEN, Chapter VIII.

✍ The vast majority are men of society. They live on the surface; they are interested in the transient and fleeting; they are like driftwood on the flood. They ask forever and only the news, the froth and scum of the eternal sea. They use policy; they make up for want of matter with manner. They have many letters to write. Wealth and the approbation of men is to them success. The enterprises of society are something final and sufficing for them. The world advises them, and they listen to its advice. They live wholly an evanescent life, creatures of circumstance. It is of prime importance to them who is the president of the day.

JOURNAL, April 24, 1852.

On Character 🌾 🌾

🌾 We falsely attribute to men a determined character; putting together all their yesterdays and averaging them, we presume to know them. Pity the man who has a character to support. It is worse than a large family.

JOURNAL, April 28, 1841.

🌾 The chief want, in every state that I have been into, was a high and earnest purpose in its inhabitants.

LIFE WITHOUT PRINCIPLE.

🌾 The world rests on principles.

LETTER TO HARRISON BLAKE, December 19, 1854.

🌾 Our least deed, like the young of the land crab, wends its way to the sea of cause and effect as soon as born, and makes a drop there to eternity.

JOURNAL, March 14, 1838.

❧   We should make a notch every day on our characters, as Robinson Crusoe on his stick. We must be at the helm at least once a day; we must feel the tiller-rope in our hands, and know that if we sail, we steer.

JOURNAL, February 22, 1841.

❧   To be a philosopher is not merely to have subtle thoughts, nor even to found a school, but so to love wisdom as to live according to its dictates, a life of simplicity, independence, magnanimity, and trust. It is to solve some of the problems of life, not only theoretically, but practically.

WALDEN, Chapter I.

❧   Why should we ever go abroad, even across the way, to ask a neighbor's advice? There is a nearer neighbor within us incessantly telling us how we should behave. But we wait for the neighbor without to tell us of some false, easier way.

LETTER TO HARRISON BLAKE, December 19, 1854.

❧   Talk of fate! How little one can know what is fated to another—what he can do and what he cannot do! I doubt whether one can give or receive any very pertinent advice.

JOURNAL, December 27, 1858.

❧   They, methinks, are poor stuff and creatures of a miserable fate who can be advised and persuaded in very important steps.

JOURNAL, December 27, 1858.

ON CHARACTER

❀ If you would convince a man that he does wrong, do right. But do not care to convince him. Men will believe what they see. Let them see.
LETTER TO HARRISON BLAKE, March 27, 1848.

❀ The outward is only the outside of that which is within. Men are not concealed under habits, but are revealed by them; they are their true clothes.
LETTER TO HARRISON BLAKE, March 27, 1848.

❀ It is an important difference between two characters that the one is satisfied with a happy but level success but the other as constantly elevates his aim. Though my life is low, if my spirit looks upward habitually at an elevated angle, it is as it were redeemed. When the desire to be better than we are is really sincere we are instantly elevated, and so far better already.
JOURNAL, 1851.

❀ Most men can be easily transplanted from here there, for they have so little root—no tap-root—or their roots penetrate so little way, that you can thrust a shovel quite under them and take them up, roots and all.
JOURNAL, May 14, 1852.

❀ It is not worth the while to let our imperfections disturb us always. The conscience really does not, and ought not to monopolize the whole of our lives, any more than the heart or the head. It is as liable to disease as any other part. I have seen some whose consciences, owing undoubtedly to former indulgence, had grown to be as irritable as spoilt children, and at length gave them no peace. They did not know when to swallow their cud, and their lives of course yielded no milk.

THE WEEK, Sunday.

Circumstances are not rigid and unyielding, but our habits are rigid.

LETTER TO HARRISON BLAKE, March 27, 1848.

You may know what a thing costs or is worth to you; you can never know what it costs or is worth to me. All the community may scream because one man is born who will not do as it does, who will not conform because conformity to him is death—he is so constituted. They know nothing about his case; they are fools when they presume to advise him. The man of genius knows what he is aiming at; nobody else knows. And he alone knows when something comes between him and his object. In the course of generations, however, men will excuse you for not doing as they do, if you will bring enough to pass in your own way.

JOURNAL, December 27, 1858.

Every man's success is in proportion to his *average* ability.

JOURNAL, 1837–47.

When we are shocked at vice we express a lingering sympathy with it. Dry rot, rust, and mildew shock no man, for none is subject to them.

JOURNAL, June 22, 1840.

ON CHARACTER

❦ It is best to lay our plans widely in youth, for then land is cheap, and it is but too easy to contract our views afterwards. Youths so laid out, with broad avenues and parks, that they may make handsome and liberal old men!

A YANKEE IN CANADA.

❦ They who are ready to go are already invited.

JOURNAL, July 2, 1840.

❦ I observe that the *New York Herald* advertises situations wanted by "respectable young women" by the column, but never by respectable young men, rather "intelligent" and "smart" ones; from which I infer that the public opinion of New York does not require young men to be respectable in the same sense in which it requires young women to be so.

JOURNAL, April 30, 1851.

❦ Of what consequence, though our planet explode, if there is no character involved in the explosion? In health we have not the least curiosity about such events. We do not live for idle amusement. I would not run round a corner to see the world blow up.

LIFE WITHOUT PRINCIPLE.

❦ Dreams are the touchstones of our characters. We are scarcely less afflicted when we remember some unworthiness in our conduct in a dream, than if it had been actual, and the intensity of our grief, which is our atonement, measures the degree by which this is separated from an actual unworthiness. For in dreams we but act a part which must have been learned and rehearsed in our waking hours, and no doubt could discover some waking consent thereto.

THE WEEK, Wednesday.

❦ I always see those of whom I have heard well with a slight disappointment.

LETTER TO RALPH W. EMERSON, June 8, 1843.

❦ We are conscious of an animal in us, which awakens in proportion as our higher nature slumbers.

WALDEN, Chapter XI.

❦ I confess, that practically speaking, when I have learned a man's real disposition, I have no hopes of changing it for the better or worse in this state of existence.

WALDEN, Chapter IV.

❦ In some cases fame is perpetually false and unjust. Or rather I should say that she *never* recognizes the simple heroism of an action, but only as connected with its apparent consequences. It praises the interested energy of the Boston Tea Party, but will be comparatively silent about the more bloody and disinterestedly heroic attack on the Boston Court-House, simply because the latter was unsuccessful. Fame is not just. It never finely discriminates praises, but coarsely hurrahs. The truest acts of heroism never reach her ear, are never published by her trumpet.

JOURNAL, June 4, 1854.

❦ There are some who never do or say anything, whose life merely excites expectation. Their excellence reaches no further than a gesture or mode of carrying themselves.

They are a sash dangling from the waist, or a sculptured war-club over the shoulder. They are like fine-edged tools gradually becoming rusty in a shop-window. I like as well, if not better, to see a piece of iron or steel, out of which many such tools will be made, or the bush-whack in a man's hand.

JOURNAL, March 10, 1859.

How often are we wise as serpents without being harmless as doves!

JOURNAL, February 9, 1851.

Men go to a fire for entertainment. When I see how eagerly men will run to a fire, whether in warm or in cold weather, by day or by night, dragging an engine at their heels, I am astonished to perceive how good a purpose the love of excitement is made to serve. What other force, pray, what offered pay, what disinterested neighborliness could ever effect so much. No, these are boys who are to be dealt with, and these are the motives that prevail. There is no old man or woman dropping into the grave but covets excitement.

JOURNAL, June 5, 1850.

It is insignificant, and a merely negative good fortune, to be provided with thick garments against cold and wet, an unprofitable, weak and defensive condition, compared with being able to extract some exhilaration, some warmth even, out of cold and wet themselves, and to clothe them with our sympathy. The rich man buys woollens and furs,

189

and sits naked and shivering still in spirit, besieged by cold and wet. But the poor Lord of Creation, cold and wet he makes to warm him, and be his garments.

JOURNAL, November 12, 1853.

❦ What was *enthusiasm* in the young man must become *temperament* in the mature man.

JOURNAL, November 1, 1851.

❦ When you travel to the Celestial City, carry no letter of introduction. When you knock, ask to see God—none of the servants.

LETTER TO HARRISON BLAKE, March 27, 1848.

❦ We can possibly *get along* with a neighbor, even with a bedfellow, whom we respect but very little; but as soon as it comes to this, that we do not respect ourselves, then we do not get along at all.

LETTER TO HARRISON BLAKE, April 10, 1853.

On Walking 🖋 🖋

🖋   It behooves us to break up this custom of sitting in the house, for it is but a custom, and I am not sure that it has the sanction of common sense. A man no sooner gets up than he sits down again.

JOURNAL, July 23, 1851.

🖋   Walden Pond was my forest walk. The English forests are divided into "walks," with a keeper presiding over each. My "walk" is ten miles from my house every way.

JOURNAL, April 12, 1852.

🖋   I set out once more to climb the mountain of the earth, for my steps are symbolical steps, and in all my walking I have not reached the top of the earth yet.

JOURNAL, March 21, 1853.

🖋   I am alarmed when it happens that I have walked a mile into the woods bodily, without getting there in spirit.

WALKING.

It is a certain faeryland where we live. You may walk out in any direction over the earth's surface, lifting your horizon, and everywhere your path, climbing the convexity of the globe, leads you between heaven and earth, not away from the light of the sun and stars and the habitations of men. I wonder that I ever get five miles on my way, the walk is so crowded with events and phenomena.

JOURNAL, June 7, 1851.

I have met with but one or two persons in the course of my life who understood the art of taking walks daily— not to exercise the legs or body merely, nor barely to recruit the spirits, but positively to exercise both body and spirit, and to succeed to the highest and worthiest ends by the abandonment of all specific ends—who had a genius, so to speak, for sauntering.

JOURNAL, January 10, 1851.

My walks were full of incidents. I attended not to the affairs of Europe, but to my own affairs in Concord fields.

JOURNAL, January 20, 1852.

I do not know how to entertain one who can't take long walks. The first thing that suggests itself is to get a horse to draw them, and that brings us at once into contact with stablers and dirty harness, and I do not get over my ride for a long time. I give up my forenoon to them and get along pretty well, the very elasticity of the air and promise of the day abetting me, but they are as heavy as dumplings by mid-afternoon. If they can't walk, why won't they take an honest nap and let me go in the afternoon?

But, come two o'clock, they alarm me by an evident disposition to sit. In the midst of the most glorious Indian-
summer afternoon, there they sit, breaking your chairs and
wearing out the house, with their backs to the light, taking
no note of the lapse of time.

JOURNAL, October 7, 1857.

Methinks I would not accept of the gift of life, if I
were required to spend as large a portion of it sitting foot
up or with my legs crossed, as the shoemakers and tailors
do. As well be tied neck and heels together and cast into
the sea.

JOURNAL, January 10, 1851.

In my afternoon walk I would fain forget all my morning occupations and my obligations to society. But it sometimes happens that I cannot easily shake off the village.
The thought of some work will run in my head and I am
not where my body is—I am out of my senses. In my walks
I would fain return to my senses. What business have I in
the woods, if I am thinking of something out of the woods?

WALKING.

This rain is good for thought. It is especially agreeable
to me as I enter the wood and hear the soothing dripping
on the leaves. It domiciles me in nature. The woods are
the more like a house for the rain; the few slight noises
sound more hollow in them; the birds hop nearer; the very
trees seem still and pensive. The clouds are but a higher
roof.

JOURNAL, May 17, 1858.

After walking by night several times I now walk by day, but I am not aware of any crowning advantage in it. I see small objects better, but it does not enlighten me any. The day is more trivial.

JOURNAL, June 15, 1851.

It requires considerable skill in crossing a country to avoid houses and too cultivated parts—somewhat of the engineer's or gunner's skill—so to pass a house, if you must go near it through high grass—pass the enemy's lines where houses are thick—as to make a hill or wood screen you—to shut every window with an apple tree. For that route which most avoids the houses is not only the one in which you will be least molested, but it is by far the most agreeable.

JOURNAL, June 19, 1852.

A turtle walking is as if a man were to try to walk by sticking his legs and arms merely out the windows.

JOURNAL, May 27, 1853.

I know of but one or two persons with whom I can afford to walk. With most the walk degenerates into a mere vigorous use of your legs, ludicrously purposeless, while you are discussing some mighty argument, each one having his say, spoiling each other's day, worrying one another with conversation, hustling one another with our conversation. I know of no use in the walking part in this case, except that we may seem to be getting on together toward some goal; but of course we keep our original distance all the way. Jumping every wall and ditch with vigor in the vain hope of shaking your companion off. Trying to kill two birds with one stone, though they sit at opposite points of the compass, to see nature and do the honors to one who does not.

JOURNAL, November 8, 1858.

🐦 And then for my afternoon walks I have a garden, larger than any artificial garden that I have read of and far more attractive to me—mile after mile of embowered walks, such as no nobleman's grounds can boast, with animals running free and wild therein as from the first— varied with land and water prospect, and, above all, so retired that it is extremely rare that I meet a single wanderer in its mazes. No gardener is seen therein. You may wander away to solitary bowers and brooks and hills.

JOURNAL, June 20, 1850.

On Business ✖ ✖

✖ I cannot *easily* buy a blank-book to write thoughts in; they are all ruled for dollars and cents.

JOURNAL, September 7, 1851.

✖ This world is a place of business. What an infinite bustle! I am awakened almost every night by the panting of the steam-engine. It interrupts my dreams. There is no sabbath. It would be glorious to see mankind at leisure for once.

JOURNAL, March 4, 1852.

✖ If a man was tossed out of a window when an infant, and so made a cripple for life, or scared out of his wits by the Indians, it is regretted chiefly because he was thus incapacitated for—business! I think that there is nothing, not even crime, more opposed to poetry, to philosophy, ay, to life itself, than this incessant business.

LIFE WITHOUT PRINCIPLE.

ON BUSINESS

As for my own business, even that kind of surveying which I could do with most satisfaction my employers do not want. They would prefer that I should do my work coarsely and not too well, ay, not well enough. When I observe that there are different ways of surveying, my employer commonly asks which will give him the most land, not which is most correct.

LIFE WITHOUT PRINCIPLE.

The momentous topics of human life are always of secondary importance to the business at hand, just as carpenters discuss politics between the strokes of the hammer while they are shingling a roof.

JOURNAL, January 23, 1841.

How trivial and uninteresting and wearisome and unsatisfactory are all employments for which men will pay you money! The ways by which you may get money all lead downward. To have done anything by which you earned money merely is to have been truly idle. If the laborer gets no more than the wages his employer pays him, he is cheated, he cheats himself.

JOURNAL, August 7, 1853.

There are certain current expressions and blasphemous moods of viewing things, as when we say "he is doing a good business," more profane than cursing and swearing. There is death and sin in such words. Let not the children hear them.

JOURNAL, April 20, 1841.

❧ You come away from the great factory saddened, as if the chief end of man were to make pails; but, in the case of the countryman who makes a few by hand, rainy days, the relative importance of human life and of pails is preserved, and you come away thinking of the simple and helpful life of the man—you do not turn pale at the thought—and would fain go to making pails yourself. We admire more the man who can use an axe or adze skillfully than him who can merely tend a machine. When labor is reduced to turning a crank it is no longer amusing nor truly profitable; but let this business become very profitable in a pecuniary sense, and so be "driven," as the phrase is, and carried on on a large scale, and the man is sunk in it, while only the pail or tray floats; we are interested in it only the the same way as the proprietor or company is.

JOURNAL, October 19, 1858.

❧ No *trade* is simple, but artificial and complex. It postpones life and substitutes death. It goes against the grain. If the first generation does not die of it, the third or fourth does.

JOURNAL, October 22, 1853.

❧ When formerly I was looking about to see what I could do for a living, some sad experience in conforming to the wishes of friends being fresh in my mind to tax my ingenuity, I thought often and seriously of picking huckleberries; that surely I could do, and its small profits might suffice—for my greatest skill has been to want but little—, so little capital is required, so little distraction from my wonted moods, I foolishly thought. While my acquaintances went unhesitatingly into trade or the professions, I contemplated this occupation as most like theirs; ranging the hills all summer to pick the berries which came in my way, and thereafter carelessly dispose of them; so to keep the flocks of Admetus. I also dreamed that I might gather the wild herbs, or carry evergreens to such villagers as loved to be reminded of the woods, even to the city, by hay-cart loads. But I have since learned that trade curses everything it handles; and though you trade in messages from heaven, the whole curse of trade attaches to the business.

WALDEN, Chapter I.

⚜ I once invented a rule for measuring cord-wood, and tried to introduce it in Boston; but the measurer there told me that the sellers did not wish to have their wood measured correctly—that he was already too accurate for them, and therefore they commonly got their wood measured in Charlestown before crossing the bridge.

LIFE WITHOUT PRINCIPLE.

⚜ Most men are engaged in business the greater part of their lives, because the soul abhors a vacuum, and they have not discovered any continuous employment for man's nobler faculties.

JOURNAL, April 27, 1854.

On Travel and Staying
at Home ❧ ❧

❧ Only that traveling is good which reveals to me the value of home and enables me to enjoy it better.

JOURNAL, March 11, 1856.

❧ He who rides and keeps the beaten track studies the fences chiefly.

THE MAINE WOODS, Chesuncook.

❧ How often it happens that the traveler's principal distinction is that he is one who knows less about the country than a native!

JOURNAL, August 6, 1851.

❧ The discoveries which we make abroad are special and particular; those which we make at home are general and significant. The further off, the nearer the surface. The nearer home, the deeper.

JOURNAL, September 7, 1851.

ON TRAVEL AND STAYING AT HOME

✻ Some do not walk at all; others walk in the highways; a few walk across lots. Roads are made for horses and men of business. I do not travel in them much, comparatively, because I am not in a hurry to get to any tavern or grocery or livery-stable or depot to which they lead.

WALKING.

✻ This is a common experience in my traveling. I plod along, thinking what a miserable world this is and what miserable fellows we that inhabit it, wondering what it is tempts men to live in it; but anon I leave the towns behind and am lost in some boundless heath, and life becomes gradually more tolerable, if not even glorious.

JOURNAL, June 17, 1857.

✻ It is far more independent to travel on foot. You have to sacrifice so much to the horse. You cannot choose the most agreeable places in which to spend the noon, commanding the finest views, because commonly there is no water there, or you cannot get there with your horse.

JOURNAL, July 4, 1858.

✻ You say that you have traveled far and wide. How many men have you seen that did not belong to any sect, or party, or clique? Did you go further than letters of introduction would avail?

JOURNAL, August 9, 1858.

✻ I have several friends and acquaintances who are very good companions in the house or for an afternoon walk, but whom I cannot make up my mind to make a longer excursion with; for I discover, all at once, that they are too gentlemanly in manners, dress, and all their habits. It is a great disadvantage for a traveler to be a gentleman of this kind; he is so ill-treated, only a prey to landlords. It would be too much of a circumstance to enter a strange town or house with such a companion. You could not travel incognito; you might get into the papers. You should travel as a common man. If such a one were to set out to make a walking-journey, he would betray himself at every step. Every one would see that he was trying an experiment, as plainly as they could see that a lame man is lame by his limping. The natives would bow to him, other gentlemen would invite him to ride, conductors would warn him that this was the second-class car, and many would take him for a clergyman; and so he would be continually pestered and balked and run upon. You would not see the natives at all. Instead of going in quietly at the back door and sitting by the kitchen fire, you would be shown into a cold parlor, there to confront a fireboard, and excite a commotion in the whole family. No, you must be a common man, or at least travel as one, and then nobody will know that you are there or have been there.

JOURNAL, June 3, 1857.

A traveler who looks at things with an impartial eye may see what the oldest inhabitant has not observed.

JOURNAL, August 20, 1851.

ON TRAVEL AND STAYING AT HOME

✄ Today you may write a chapter on the advantages of traveling, and tomorrow you may write another chapter on the advantages of not traveling.

JOURNAL, November 11, 1851.

✄ It takes a man of genius to travel in his own country, in his native village; to make any progress between his door and his gate.

JOURNAL, August 6, 1851.

✄ When you are starting away, leaving your more familiar fields, for a little adventure like a walk, you look at every object with a traveler's, or at least with historical, eyes; you pause on the first bridge, where an ordinary walk hardly commences, and begin to observe and moralize like a traveler. It is worth the while to see your native village thus sometimes, as if you were a traveler passing through it, commenting on your neighbors as strangers.

JOURNAL, September 4, 1851.

✄ A man must generally get away some hundreds or thousands of miles from home before he can be said to begin his travels. Why not begin his travels at home? Would he have to go far or look very closely to discover novelties? The traveler who, in this sense, pursues his travels at home, has the advantage at any rate of a long residence in the country to make his observations correct and profitable. Now the American goes to England, while the Englishman comes to America, in order to describe the country.

JOURNAL, August 6, 1851.

✻ There would be this advantage in traveling in your own country, even in your own neighborhood, that you would be so thoroughly prepared to understand what you saw you would make fewer traveler's mistakes.

JOURNAL, June 12, 1851.

✻ If a man is rich and strong anywhere, it must be on his native soil. Here I have been these forty years learning the language of these fields that I may the better express myself. If I should travel to the prairies, I should much less understand them, and my past life would serve me but ill to describe them. Many a weed here stands for more of life to me than the big trees of California would if I should go there. We need only travel enough to give our intellects an airing.

JOURNAL, November 20, 1857.

✻ When it was proposed to me to go abroad, rub off some rust, and *better my condition* in a worldly sense, I fear lest my life will lose some of its homeliness. If these fields and streams and woods, the phenomena of nature here, and the simple occupations of the inhabitants should cease to interest and inspire me, no culture or wealth would atone for the loss.

JOURNAL, March 11, 1856.

✻ As I sail the unexplored sea of Concord, many a dell and swamp and wooded hill is my Ceram and Amboyna.

JOURNAL, November 23, 1860.

✻ I cannot but regard it as a kindness in those who have the steering of me that, by the want of pecuniary wealth, I have been nailed down to this my native region so long and steadily, and made to study and love this spot of earth more and more. What would signify in comparison a thin and diffused love and knowledge of the whole earth instead, got by wandering? The traveler's is but a barren and comfortless condition. Wealth will not buy a man a home in nature—house nor farm there. The man of business does not by his business earn a residence in nature, but is denaturalized rather.

JOURNAL, November 12, 1853.

We have advanced by leaps to the Pacific, and left many a lesser Oregon and California unexplored behind us.

THE MAINE WOODS, Ktaadn.

If Paris is much in your mind, if it is more and more to you, Concord is less and less, and yet it would be a wretched bargain to accept the proudest Paris in exchange for my native village. At best, Paris could only be a school in which to learn to live here, a stepping-stone to Concord, a school in which to fit for this university.

JOURNAL, March 11, 1856.

How many things can you go away from? They see the comet from the northwest coast just as plainly as we do, and the same stars through its tail. Take the shortest way round and stay at home. A man dwells in his native valley like a corolla in its calyx, like an acorn in its cup. *Here,* of course, is all that you love, all that you expect, all that you are. Here is your bride elect, as close to you as she can be got. Here is all the best and all the worst you can imagine. What more do you want? Bear here-away then! Foolish people imagine that what they imagine is somewhere else. That stuff is not made in any factory but your own.

JOURNAL, November 1, 1858.

Give me the old familiar walk, postoffice and all, with this ever new self, with this infinite expectation and faith, which does not know when it is beaten. We'll go nutting once more. We'll pluck the nut of the world, and crack it in the winter evenings. Theaters and all other sightseeing are puppet-shows in comparison. I will take another walk to the Cliff, another row on the river, another skate on the meadow, be out in the first snow, and associate with the winter birds. Here I am at home. In the bare and bleached crust of the earth I recognize my friend.

JOURNAL, November 1, 1858.

I want nothing new, if I can have but a tithe of the old secured to me. I will spurn all wealth beside. Think of the consummate folly of attempting to go away from *here!* When the constant endeavor should be to get nearer and nearer *here!*

JOURNAL, November 1, 1858.

On Wisdom * *

❊ A wise man sees as clearly the heathenism and barbarity of his own countrymen as those of the nations to whom his countrymen send missionaries.

JOURNAL, January 16, 1852.

❊ It is strange that men are in such haste to get fame as teachers rather than knowledge as learners.

JOURNAL, March 11, 1856.

❊ Men do not fail commonly for want of knowledge, but for want of prudence to give wisdom the preference.

THE WEEK, Monday.

❊ The title *wise* is, for the most part, falsely applied. How can one be a wise man, if he does not know any better how to live than other men?

LIFE WITHOUT PRINCIPLE.

✳ Woe be to the generation that lets any higher faculty in its midst go unemployed!

JOURNAL, December 22, 1853.

✳ We have heard of a Society for the Diffusion of Useful Knowledge. It is said that knowledge is power, and the like. Methinks there is equal need of a Society for the Diffusion of Useful Ignorance, what we call Beautiful Knowledge, a knowledge in a higher sense: for what is most of our boasted so-called knowledge but a conceit that we know something, which robs us of the advantage of our actual ignorance? What we call knowledge is often our positive ignorance; ignorance our negative knowledge.

WALKING.

✳ A man's ignorance sometimes is not only useful, but beautiful—while his knowledge, so called, is oftentimes worse than useless, besides being ugly. Which is the best man to deal with—he who knows nothing about a subject, and, what is extremely rare, knows that he knows nothing, or he who really knows something about it, but thinks that he knows all?

WALKING.

✳ A man is wise with the wisdom of his time only, and ignorant with its ignorance. Observe how the greatest minds yield in some degree to the superstitions of their age.

JOURNAL, January 31, 1853.

❋   I do not know that I am very fond of novelty. I wish to get a clearer notion of what I have already some inkling.

JOURNAL, August 6, 1851.

❋   I am, perchance, most and most profitably interested in the things which I already know a little about; a mere and utter novelty is a mere monstrosity to me.

JOURNAL, August 6, 1851.

❋   I fear that the character of my knowledge is from year to year becoming more distinct and scientific; that, in exchange for views as wide as heaven's cope, I am being narrowed down to the field of the microscope. I see details, not wholes nor the shadow of the whole. I count some parts, and say, "I know."

JOURNAL, August 19, 1851.

❋   How few things can a man measure with the tape of his understanding!

JOURNAL, February 14, 1851.

❋   I find it to be the height of wisdom not to endeavor to oversee myself and live a life of prudence and common sense, but to see over and above myself, entertain sublime conjectures, to make myself the thoroughfare of thrilling thoughts, live all that can be lived.

JOURNAL, November 23, 1850.

❋ Who shall distinguish between the *law* by which a brook finds its river, the *instinct* by which a bird performs its migrations, and the *knowledge* by which a man steers his ship around the globe? The globe is the richer for the variety of its inhabitants.

JOURNAL, *May 17, 1854.*

❋ The community has no bribe that will tempt a wise man. You may raise money enough to tunnel a mountain, but you cannot raise enough to hire a man who is minding *his own* business.

LIFE WITHOUT PRINCIPLE.

❋ Where the good husbandman is, there is the good soil.

JOURNAL, *April 24, 1859.*

❋ Man needs to know but little more than a lobster in order to catch him in his traps.

CAPE COD, *Chapter X.*

❋ Why level down to our dullest perception always, and praise that as common sense? The commonest sense is the sense of men asleep, which they express by snoring.

WALDEN, *Chapter XVIII.*

❋ We are acquainted with a mere pellicle of the globe on which we live. Most have not delved six feet beneath the surface, nor leaped as many above it. We know not where we are. Beside, we are sound asleep nearly half our time.

WALDEN, *Chapter XVIII.*

On Solitude ✍ ✍

✍ It would be better if there were but one inhabitant to a square mile, as where I live.

WALDEN, Chapter V.

✍ I find it wholesome to be alone the greater part of the time. To be in company, even with the best, is soon wearisome and dissipating. I love to be alone. I never found the companion that was so companionable as solitude. We are for the most part more lonely when we go abroad among men than when we stay in our chambers. A man thinking or working is always alone, let him be where he will. Solitude is not measured by the miles of space that intervene between a man and his fellows.

WALDEN, Chapter V.

✍ By my intimacy with nature I find myself withdrawn from man. My interest in the sun and the moon, in the morning and the evening, compels me to solitude.

JOURNAL, July 26, 1852.

🖉 I have never felt lonesome, or in the least oppressed by a sense of solitude, but once, and that was a few weeks after I came to the woods, when, for an hour, I doubted if the near neighborhood of man was not essential to a serene and healthy life. To be alone was something unpleasant. But I was at the same time conscious of a slight insanity in my mood, and seemed to foresee my recovery.

WALDEN, Chapter V.

🖉 I am no more lonely than the loon in the pond that laughs so loud, or than Walden Pond itself. I am no more lonely than a single mullein or dandelion in a pasture, or a bean leaf, or sorrel, or a horsefly, or a humblebee. I am no more lonely than the Mill Brook, or a weathercock, or the north star, or the south wind, or an April shower, or a January thaw, or the first spider in a new house.

WALDEN, Chapter V.

🖉 You think that I am impoverishing myself by withdrawing from men, but in my solitude I have woven for myself a silken web or *chrysalis,* and, nymph-like, shall ere long burst forth a more perfect creature, fitted for a higher society.

JOURNAL, February 8, 1857.

🖉 I thrive best on solitude. If I have had a companion only one day in a week, unless it were one or two I could name, I find that the value of the week to me has been seriously affected. It dissipates my days, and often it takes me another week to get over it.

JOURNAL, December 28, 1856.

ON SOLITUDE

🖉 What sort of space is that which separates a man from his fellows and makes him solitary? I have found that no exertion of the legs can bring two minds much nearer to one another. What do we want most to dwell near to? Not to many men surely, the depot, the post-office, the bar-room, the meeting-house, the school-house, the grocery, Beacon Hill, or the Five Points, where men most congregate, but to the perennial source of our life, whence in all our experience we have found that to issue, as the willow stands near the water and sends out its roots in that direction. This will vary with different natures, but this is the place where a wise man will dig his cellar.

WALDEN, Chapter V.

🖉 I never chanced to meet with any man so cheering and elevating and encouraging, so infinitely suggestive, as the stillness and solitude of the Well Meadow Field.

JOURNAL, January 11, 1857.

🖉 I have an immense appetite for solitude, like an infant for sleep, and if I don't get enough of it this year, I shall cry all the next.

LETTER TO DANIEL RICKETSON, September 9, 1857.

🖉 Some of my pleasantest hours were during the long rain-storms in the spring or fall, which confined me to the house for the afternoon as well as the forenoon, soothed by their ceaseless roar and pelting; when an early twilight ushered in a long evening in which many thoughts had time to take root and unfold themselves.

WALDEN, Chapter V.

✍ I do not know if I am singular when I say that I believe there is no man with whom I can associate who will not, comparatively speaking, spoil my afternoon. That society or encounter may at last yield a fruit which I am not aware of, but I cannot help suspecting that I should have spent those hours more profitably alone.

JOURNAL, November 25, 1857.

✍ Mrs. A takes on dolefully on account of the solitude in which she lives, but she gets little consolation. Mrs. B says she envies her that retirement. Mrs. A is aware that she does, and says it is as if a thirsty man should envy another the river in which he is drowning. So goes the world. It is either this extreme or that. Of solitude one gets too much and another not enough.

JOURNAL, March 11, 1859.

✍ I have a great deal of company in my house; especially in the morning, when nobody calls.

WALDEN, Chapter V.

✍ It is surprising how much room there is in nature— if a man will follow his proper path. In these broad fields, in these extensive woods, on this stretching river, I never meet a walker. Passing behind the farmhouses, I see no man out. Perhaps I do not meet so many men as I should have met three centuries ago, when the Indian hunter roamed these woods. I enjoy the retirement and solitude of an early settler. Men have cleared some of the earth, which no doubt is an advantage to the walker. I see a man sometimes chopping in the woods, or planting or hoeing in a field, at a distance; and yet there may be a lyceum in the evening, and there is a bookshop and library in the village, and five times a day I can be whirled to Boston within an hour.

JOURNAL, January 26, 1853.

🖋 I have found myself as well off when I have fallen into a quagmire, as in an armchair in the most hospitable house. The prospect was pretty much the same. Without anxiety let us wander on, admiring whatever beauty the woods exhibit.

JOURNAL, 1850.

🖋 There is no better fence to put between you and the village than a storm into which the villagers do not venture out.

JOURNAL, March 8, 1859.

🖋 Ah! I need solitude. I have come forth to this hill at sunset to see the forms of the mountains in the horizon— to behold and commune with something grander than man. Their mere distance and unprofanedness is an infinite encouragement. It is with infinite yearning and aspiration that I seek solitude, more and more resolved and strong; but with a certain genial weakness that I seek society ever.

JOURNAL, August 14, 1854.

🖋 I have lately got back to that glorious society called Solitude.

LETTER TO HARRISON BLAKE, January 1, 1859.

On Manners
and Fashion 🌿 🌿

🌿 One man lies in his words and gets a bad reputation; another in his manners, and enjoys a good one.
JOURNAL, June 25, 1852.

🌿 My neighbor does not recover from his formal bow so soon as I do from the pleasure of meeting him.
JOURNAL, February 16, 1851.

🌿 It is not the invitation which I hear, but which I feel, that I obey.
JOURNAL, April 22, 1851.

🌿 Manners are conscious; character is unconscious.
JOURNAL, February 16, 1851.

🌿 The man who thrusts his manners upon me does as if he were to insist on introducing me to his cabinet of curiosities, when I wished to see himself.
LIFE WITHOUT PRINCIPLES.

ON MANNERS AND FASHION

✤ With many men their fine manners are a lie all over, a skim-coat or finish of falsehood. They are not brave enough to do without this sort of armor, which they wear night and day.

JOURNAL, March 29, 1858.

✤ The vice of manners is that they are continually deserted by the character; they are cast-off clothes or shells, claiming the respect of the living creature.

JOURNAL, February 16, 1851.

✤ I have always found that what is called the best of manners are the worst, for they are simply the shell without the meat. They cover no life at all. *They* are the universal slaveholders, who treat men as things. Nobody holds you more cheap than the man of manners. They are marks by the help of which the wearers ignore you and remain concealed themselves. Are they such great characters that they feel obliged to make the journey of life incognito? Sailors swear; gentlemen make their manners to you.

JOURNAL, October 4, 1859.

✤ It appears to me that a true Englishman can only speculate within bounds; he has to pay his respects to so many things that before he knows it he has paid all he is worth.

JOURNAL, August 21, 1851.

❀ It is possible for a man wholly to disappear and be merged in his manners. The thousand and one gentlemen whom I meet, I meet despairingly and but to part from them, for I am not cheered by the hope of any rudeness from them.

JOURNAL, July 21, 1851.

❀ Men are very generally spoiled by being so civil and well-disposed. You can have no profitable conversation with them, they are so conciliatory, determined to agree with you.

JOURNAL, July 21, 1851.

❀ I would not have every man cultivated, any more than I would have every acre of earth cultivated. Some must be preparing a mould by the annual decay of the forests which they sustain.

JOURNAL, February 13, 1851.

❀ Compliments and flattery oftenest excite my contempt by the pretension they imply, for who is he that assumes to flatter me? To compliment often implies an assumption of superiority in the complimenter. It is, in fact, a subtle detraction.

JOURNAL, March 27, 1857.

❀ There is the world-wide fact that, from the mass of men, the appearance of wealth, dress, and equipage alone command respect. They who yield it are the heathen who need to have missionaries sent to them.

JOURNAL, January 17, 1852.

ON MANNERS AND FASHION

❦ It is astonishing how far a merely well-dressed and good-looking man may go without being challenged by any sentinel.

JOURNAL, January 3, 1856.

❦ When I see a fine lady or gentleman dressed to the top of the fashion, I wonder what they would do if an earthquake should happen, or a fire suddenly break out, for they seem to have counted only on fair weather, and that things will go on smoothly and without jostling.

JOURNAL, July 12, 1840.

❦ The walker and naturalist does not wear a hat, or a shoe, or a coat, to be looked at, but for other uses. When a citizen comes to take a walk with me I commonly find that he is lame—disabled by his shoeing. He is sure to wet his feet, tear his coat, and jam his hat, and the superior quality of my boots, coat, and hat appear. I once went into the woods with a party for a fortnight. I wore my old and common clothes, which were of Vermont gray. They wore, no doubt, the best they had for such an occasion—of a fashionable color and quality. I thought that they were a little ashamed of me while we were in the towns. They all tore their clothes badly but myself, and I, who, it chanced, was the only one provided with needles and thread, enabled them to mend them. When we came out of the woods I was the best dressed of any of them.

JOURNAL, March 26, 1860.

❧ When I go a-visiting I find that I go off the fashionable street—not being inclined to change my dress—to where man meets man and not polished shoe meets shoe.

JOURNAL, June 11, 1855.

❧ I just had a coat come home from the tailor's. Ah me! Who am I that I should wear this coat? It was fitted upon one of the devil's angels about my size. Of what use that measuring of me if he did not measure my character, but only the breadth of my shoulders, as if it were a peg to hang it on. This is not the figure that I cut. This is the figure the tailor cuts.

JOURNAL, January 14, 1854.

❧ Ladies are in haste to dress *as if* it were cold or *as if* it were warm—though it may not yet be so—merely to display a new dress.

JOURNAL, December 25, 1859.

❧ We worship not the Graces, nor the Parcae, but Fashion. She spins and weaves and cuts with full authority. The head monkey at Paris puts on a traveler's cap, and all the monkeys in America do the same.

WALDEN, Chapter I.

On Waters 🐚 🐚

🐚 A lake is the landscape's most beautiful and expressive feature. It is earth's eye; looking into which the beholder measures the depth of his own nature. The fluviatile trees next the shore are the slender eyelashes which fringe it, and the wooded hills and cliffs around are its overhanging brows.

WALDEN, Chapter IX.

🐚 Of all the characters I have known, perhaps Walden wears best, and best preserves its purity. Many men have been likened to it, but few deserve that honor.

WALDEN, Chapter IX.

🐚 When I was four years old, as I well remember, I was brought from Boston to this my native town, through these very woods and this field, to the pond. It is one of the oldest scenes stamped on my memory. And now tonight my flute has waked the echoes over that very water. The pines still stand here older than I; or, if some have fallen, I have cooked my supper with their stumps, and a new growth is rising all around, preparing another aspect for new infant eyes.

WALDEN, Chapter VII.

A field of water betrays the spirit that is in the air. It is continually receiving new life and motion from above. It is intermediate in its nature between land and sky. On land only the grass and trees wave, but the water itself is rippled by the wind.

WALDEN, Chapter IX.

Nothing so fair, so pure, and at the same time so large, as a lake, perchance, lies on the surface of the earth. Sky water. It needs no fence. Nations come and go without defiling it. It is a mirror which no stone can crack, whose quicksilver will never wear off, whose gild-ing Nature continually repairs; no storms, no dust, can dim its surface ever fresh—a mirror in which all impurity presented to it sinks, swept and dusted by the sun's hazy brush—this the light dust-cloth—which retains no breath that is breathed on it, but sends its own to float as clouds high above its surface, and be reflected in its bosom still.

WALDEN, Chapter IX.

Every winter the liquid and trembling surface of the pond, which was so sensitive to every breath, and re-flected every light and shadow, becomes solid to the depth of a foot or a foot and a half, so that it will support the heaviest teams, and perchance the snow covers it to an equal depth, and it is not to be distinguished from any level field. Like the marmots in the surrounding hills, it closes its eyelids and becomes dormant for three months or more.

WALDEN, Chapter XVI.

The seashore is a sort of neutral ground, a most advantageous point from which to contemplate this world. It is even a trivial place. The waves forever rolling to the land are too far-traveled and untamable to be familiar.

CAPE COD, Chapter IX.

Though once there were more whales cast up here, I think that it was never more wild than now. We do not associate the idea of antiquity with the ocean, nor wonder how it looked a thousand years ago, as we do of the land, for it was equally wild and unfathomable always. The Indians have left no traces on its surface, but it is the same to the civilized man and the savage. The aspect of the shore only has changed. The ocean is a wilderness reaching round the globe, wilder than a Bengal jungle, and fuller of monsters, washing the very wharves of our cities and the gardens of our seaside residences. Serpents, bears, hyenas, tigers rapidly vanish as civilization advances, but the most populous and civilized city cannot scare a shark far from its wharves.

CAPE COD, Chapter IX.

Ladies who never walk in the woods, sail over the sea. To go to the sea! Why, it is to have the experience of Noah—to realize the deluge. Every vessel is an ark.

CAPE COD, Chapter IX.

We are made to love the river and the meadow, as the wind to ripple the water.

JOURNAL, *February 14, 1851.*

For the first time it occurred to me this afternoon what a piece of wonder a river is—a huge volume of matter ceaselessly rolling through the fields and meadows of this substantial earth, making haste from the high places, by stable dwellings of men and Egyptian Pyramids, to its restless reservoir. One would think that, by a very natural impulse, the dwellers upon the headwaters of the Mississippi and Amazon would follow in the trail of their waters to see the end of the matter.

JOURNAL, *September 5, 1838.*

The river is my own highway, the only wild and unfenced part of the world hereabouts.

JOURNAL, *May 30, 1852.*

Without being owner of any land, I find that I have a civil right in the river—that, if I am not a land-owner I am a water-owner. It is fitting, therefore, that I should have a boat, a cart, for this my farm. Since it is almost wholly given up to a few of us, while the other highways are much traveled, no wonder that I improve it. Such a one as I will choose to dwell in a township where there are most ponds and rivers and our range is widest. In relation to the river, I find my natural rights least infringed on. It is an extensive "common" still left.

JOURNAL, *March 23, 1853.*

🦑 I think that I speak impartially when I say that I have never met with a stream so suitable for boating and botanizing as the Concord, and fortunately nobody knows it. I know of reaches which a single country-seat would spoil beyond remedy, but there has not been any important change here since I can remember. The willows slumber along its shore, piled in light but low masses, even like the cumuli clouds above. We pass haymakers in every meadow, who may think that we are idlers. But Nature takes care that every nook and crevice is explored by some one. While they look after the open meadows, we farm the tract between the river's brinks and behold the shores from that side. We, too, are harvesting an annual crop with our eyes, and think you Nature is not glad to display her beauty to us?

JOURNAL, August 6, 1858.

🦑 It is pleasant to embark on a voyage, if only for a short river excursion, the boat to be your home for the day, especially if it is neat and dry. A sort of moving studio it becomes, you can carry so many things with you. It is almost as if you put oars out at your windows and moved your house along.

JOURNAL, August 31, 1852.

🦑 Set sail homeward about an hour before sundown. The breeze blows me glibly across Fair Haven, the last dying gale of the day. No wonder men love to be sailors, to be blown about the world sitting at the helm, to shave

the capes and see the islands disappear under their sterns
—gubernators to a piece of wood. It disposes to contemplation, and is to me instead of smoking.

JOURNAL, August 30, 1853.

A river touching the back of a town is like a wing,
it may be unused as yet, but ready to waft it over the
world. With its rapid current it is a slightly fluttering
wing. River towns are winged towns.

JOURNAL, July 2, 1858.

Rivers, too, like the walker, unbutton their icy coats,
and we see the dark bosoms of their channels in the midst
of the ice.

JOURNAL, March 10, 1859.

The architect of the river builds with sand chiefly,
not with mud. Mud is deposited very slowly, only in the
stagnant places, but sand is the ordinary building-
material.

JOURNAL, July 19, 1859.

Again, rivers appear to have traveled back and worn
into the meadows of their creating, and then they become
more meandering than ever. Thus in the course of ages
the rivers wriggle in their beds, till it feels comfortable
under them.

JOURNAL, March 24, 1855.

What can be more impressive than to look up a
noble river just at evening—one, perchance, which you
have never explored—and behold its placid waters, re-

flecting the woods and sky, lapsing inaudibly toward the ocean; to behold as a lake, but know it as a river, tempting the beholder to explore it and his own destiny at once?

JOURNAL, July 9, 1851.

Rivers must have been the guides which conducted the footsteps of the first travelers. They are the constant lure, when they flow by our doors, to distant enterprise and adventure; and, by a natural impulse, the dwellers on their banks will at length accompany their currents to the lowlands of the globe, or explore at their invitation the interior of continents. They are the natural highways of all nations, not only leveling the ground and removing obstacles from the path of the traveler, quenching his thirst and bearing him on their bosoms, but conducting him through the most interesting scenery, the most populous portions of the globe, and where the animal and vegetable kingdoms attain their greatest perfection.

THE WEEK, Concord River.

This Sunday ended by the going down of the sun, leaving us still on the waves. But they who are on the water enjoy a longer and brighter twilight than they who are on the land, for here the water, as well as the atmosphere, absorbs and reflects the light, and some of the day seems to have sunk down into the waves. The light gradually forsook the deep water, as well as the deeper air, and the gloaming came to the fishes as well as to us, and more dim and gloomy to them, whose day is a perpetual twilight, though sufficiently bright for their weak and watery eyes. Vespers had already rung in many a dim and watery chapel down below, where the shadows of the weeds were extended in length over the sandy floor. The vespertinal pout had already begun to flit on leathern fin, and the finny gossips withdrew from the fluvial street to creeks and coves, and other private haunts, excepting a few of stronger fin, which anchored in the stream, stemming the tide even in their dreams. Meanwhile, like a dark evening cloud, we were wafted over the cope of their sky, deepening the shadows on their deluged fields.

THE WEEK, Sunday.

A single boatman passing up or down unavoidably shakes the whole of a wide river, and disturbs its every reflection.

JOURNAL, September, 1850.

On Cities ⚔ ⚔

⚔ Coming out of town—willingly as usual . . .

JOURNAL, July 9, 1851.

⚔ When I go to Boston, I naturally go straight through the city (taking the Market in my way) down to the end of Long Wharf, and look off—for I have no cousins in the back alleys—and there I see a great many countrymen in their shirt-sleeves from Maine and Pennsylvania, and all along the shore and in shore, and some foreigners beside, loading and unloading and steering their teams about, as at a country fair.

CAPE COD, Chapter X.

⚔ The village is the place to which the roads tend, a sort of expansion of the highway, as a lake of a river.

WALKING.

❊ I don't like the city better, the more I see of it. The pigs in the street are the most respectable part of the population. When will the world learn that a million men are of no importance compared with _one_ man?

LETTER TO R. W. EMERSON FROM NEW YORK, June 8, 1843.

❊ I will be a countryman. I will not go to the city, even in winter, any more than the sallows and sweet-gale by the river do.

JOURNAL, January 30, 1854.

❊ When I go through a village, my legs ache at the prospect of the hard gravelled walk. I go by the tavern with its porch full of gazers, and meet a miss taking a walk or the doctor in his sulky, and for half an hour I feel as strange as if I were in a town in China; but soon I am at home in the wide world again, and my feet rebound from the yielding turf.

JOURNAL, June 16, 1857.

❊ It is folly to attempt to educate children within a city; the first step must be to remove them out of it.

JOURNAL, July 25, 1851.

❊ Great piles of goods and the means of packing and conveying them, much wrapping paper and twine, many crates and hogsheads and trucks, that is Boston. The more barrels, the more Boston. The museums and scientific societies and libraries are accidental.

JOURNAL, December 25, 1853.

230

On Observation ✳ ✳

✳ The question is not what you look at, but what you see.

JOURNAL, August 5, 1851.

✳ We must look a long time before we can see.
NATURAL HISTORY OF MASSACHUSETTS.

✳ Many an object is not seen, though it falls within the range of our visual ray, because it does not come within the range of our intellectual ray, i.e. we are not looking for it. So, in the largest sense, we find only the world we look for.

JOURNAL, July 2, 1857.

✳ Nature does not cast pearls before swine. There is just as much beauty visible to us in the landscape as we are prepared to appreciate—not a grain more. The actual objects which one person will see from a particular hill-

top are just as different from those which another will
see as the persons are different.

JOURNAL, November 4, 1858.

❅ Take one of our selectmen and put him on the highest hill in the township, and tell him to look! What, probably, would he see? What would he *select* to look at?
Sharpening his sight to the utmost, and putting on the
glasses that suited him best, aye, using a spyglass if he
liked, straining his optic nerve to the utmost, and making
a full report. Of course, he would see a Brocken spectre
of himself. Now take Julius Caesar, or Emanuel Sweden-
borg, or a Fiji-Islander, and set him up there! Let them
compare notes afterward. Would it appear that they had
enjoyed the same prospect? For aught we know, as
strange a man as any of these is always at our elbows. It
does not appear that anybody saw Shakespeare when he
was about in England looking off, but only some of his
raiment.

JOURNAL, November 4, 1858.

❅ You might say of a philosopher that he was in this
world as a spectator.

JOURNAL, 1850.

❅ How differently the poet and the naturalist look at
objects! A man sees only what concerns him. A botanist
absorbed in the pursuit of grasses does not distinguish
the grandest pasture oaks. He as it were tramples down
oaks unwittingly in his walk.

JOURNAL, September 9, 1858.

❋ I have the habit of attention to such excess that my senses get no rest, but suffer from a constant strain. Be not preoccupied with looking. Go not to the object; let it come to you. When I have found myself ever looking down and confining my gaze to the flowers, I have thought it might be well to get into the habit of observing the clouds as a corrective; but no! that study would be just as bad. What I need is not to look at all, but a true sauntering of the eye.

JOURNAL, September 13, 1852.

❋ Could a greater miracle take place than for us to look through each other's eyes for an instant?

WALDEN, Chapter I.

❋ We are not wont to see our dooryard as a part of the earth's surface. The gardener does not perceive that some ridge or mound in his garden or lawn is related to yonder hill or the still more distant mountain in the horizon, is, perchance, a humble spur of the last.

JOURNAL, November 1, 1858.

❋ Most that is first written on any subject is a mere groping after it, mere rubble-stone and foundation. It is only when many observations of different periods have been brought together that he begins to grasp his subject and can make one pertinent and just observation.

JOURNAL, February 3, 1859.

❋ From the mountains we do not discern our native hills; but from our native hills we look out easily to the far blue mountains, which seem to preside over them. As I look northwestward to that summit from a Concord cornfield, how little can I realize all the life that is passing between me and it—the retired up-country farmhouses, the lonely mills, wooded vales, wild rocky pastures, and new clearings on stark mountainsides, and rivers murmuring through primitive woods! All these, and how much more, I *overlook*. I see the very peak—there can be no mistake—but how much I do not see, that is between me and it!

JOURNAL, September 27, 1852.

❋ When the far mountains are invisible, the near ones look the higher.

JOURNAL, 1850.

❋ All distant landscapes seen from hilltops are veritable pictures, which will be found to have no actual existence to him who travels to them.

JOURNAL, May 1, 1851.

❋ Sometimes I would rather get a transient glimpse or side view of a thing than stand fronting to it—as these polypodies. The object I caught a glimpse of as I went by haunts my thoughts a long time, is infinitely suggestive, and I do not care to front it and scrutinize it, for I know that the thing that really concerns me is not there, but in my relation to that.

JOURNAL, November 5, 1857.

❋ As you *see*, so at length will you *say*.

JOURNAL, November 1, 1851.

❊ Why not take more elevated and broader views, walk in the greater garden, not sulk in a little "debauched" nook of it? Consider the beauty of the earth, and not merely a few impounded herbs? However, you will not see these splendors, whether you stand on the hilltop or in the hollow, unless you are prepared to see them. The gardener can see only the gardener's garden, wherever he goes. The beauty of the earth answers exactly to your demand and appreciation.

JOURNAL, November 2, 1858.

❊ If there is something that does not concern me, which is out of my line, which by experience or by genius my attention is not drawn to, however novel and remarkable it may be, if it is spoken, we hear it not, if it is written, we read it not, or if we read it, it does not detain us. Every man thus *tracks himself* through life, in all his hearing and reading and observation and traveling. His observations make a chain. The phenomenon or fact that cannot in any wise be linked with the rest which he has observed, he does not observe. By and by we may be ready to receive what we cannot receive now.

JOURNAL, January 5, 1860.

❊ A man has not seen a thing who has not felt it.

JOURNAL, February 23, 1860.

❊ Not only different objects are presented to our attention at different seasons of the year, but we are in a frame of body and of mind to appreciate different objects at different seasons. I see one thing when it is cold and another when it is warm.

JOURNAL, November 17, 1858.

❋ Many a man, when I tell him that I have been onto a mountain, asks if I took a glass with me. No doubt I could have seen further with a glass, and particular objects more distinctly—could have counted more meeting-houses; but this has nothing to do with the peculiar beauty and grandeur of the view which an elevated position affords. It was not to see a few particular objects, as if they were near at hand, as I had been accustomed to see them, that I ascended the mountain, but to see an infinite variety far and near in their relation to each other, thus reduced to a single picture.

JOURNAL, October 20, 1852.

❋ All things in this world must be seen with the morning dew on them, must be seen with youthful, early-opened, hopeful eyes.

JOURNAL, June 13, 1852.

❋ Fishermen, hunters, wood-choppers and others, spending their lives in the fields and woods, in a peculiar sense a part of Nature themselves, are often in a more favorable mood for observing her, in the intervals of their pursuits, than philosophers or poets even, who approach her with expectation.

WALDEN, Chapter XI.

❋ Flowers were made to be seen, not overlooked. Their bright colors imply eyes, spectators.

JOURNAL, June 15, 1852.

❋ Every flower and weed has its day in the medical pharmacopoeia, but the beauty of flowers is perennial in the taste of men.

JOURNAL, October 13, 1860.

❋ The sunset sky reached quite from west to east, and it was the most varied in its forms and colors of any that I remember to have seen. At one time the clouds were most softly and delicately rippled, like the ripple-marks on sand. But it was hard for me to see its beauty then, when my mind was filled with Captain Brown. So great a wrong as his fate implied overshadowed all the beauty in the world.

JOURNAL, November 12, 1859.

❋ That virtue we appreciate is as much ours as another's. We see so much only as we possess.

JOURNAL, June 22, 1839.

❋ A farmer told me in all sincerity that, having occasion to go into Walden Woods in his sleigh, he thought he never saw anything so beautiful in all his life, and if there had been men there who knew how to write about it, it would have been a great occasion for them.

JOURNAL, January 18, 1859.

❋ I am always struck by the centrality of the observer's position. He always stands fronting the middle of the arch, and does not suspect at first that a thousand observers on a thousand hills behold the sunset sky from equally favorable positions.

JOURNAL, July 10, 1851.

237

THE THOUGHTS OF THOREAU

❋ Praise begins when things are seen partially. We begin to praise when we begin to see that a thing needs our assistance.

JOURNAL, June 20, 1840.

❋ If I wished to see a mountain or other scenery under the most favorable auspices, I would go to it in foul weather, so as to be there when it cleared up; we are then in the most suitable mood, and nature is most fresh and inspiring. There is no serenity so fair as that which is just established in a tearful eye.

THE MAINE WOODS, Allegash.

❋ It is impossible for the same person to see things from the poet's point of view and that of the man of science. The poet's second love may be science, not his first—when use has worn off the bloom. I realize that men may be born to a condition of mind at which others arrive in middle age by the decay of their poetic faculties.

JOURNAL, February 18, 1852.

❋ I must walk more with free senses. It is as bad to study stars and clouds as flowers and stones. I must let my senses wander as my thoughts, my eyes see without looking. Carlyle said that how to observe was to look, but I say that it is rather to see, and the more you look the less you will observe.

JOURNAL, September 13, 1852.

On Education ✠ ✠

✠ What does education often do? It makes a straight-cut ditch of a free, meandering brook.

JOURNAL, 1850.

✠ We of Massachusetts boast a good deal of what we do for the education of our people, of our district-school system; and yet our district schools are as it were but infant-schools, and we have no system for the education of the great mass who are grown up.

JOURNAL, September 27, 1851.

✠ We boast that we belong to the Nineteenth Century, and are making the most rapid strides of any nation. But consider how little this village does for its own culture. We have a comparatively decent system of common schools, schools for infants only, as it were, but, except-ing the half-starved Lyceum in the winter, no schools for ourselves. It is time that we had uncommon schools, that we did not leave off our education when we begin to be men.

JOURNAL, August 29, 1852.

Many go to Europe *to finish their education*, and when they have returned their friends remark that the most they have acquired is a correct pronunciation of English. It is a premature hardening but hollowing of the shell. They become valuable utensils of the gourd kind, but have no palatable and nutritious inside. Instead of acquiring nutritious and palatable qualities to their pulp, it is all absorbed into a prematurely hardened shell. They went away squashes, and they return gourds. They are all expressed, or squeezed out; their essential oil is gone.

JOURNAL, July 30, 1853.

It is remarkable that no pains is taken to teach children to distinguish colors. I am myself uncertain about the names of many.

JOURNAL, January 28, 1852.

Do not think that the fruits of New England are mean and insignificant, while those of some foreign land are noble and memorable. Our own, whatever they may be, are far more important to us than any others can be. They educate us, and fit us to live in New England. Better for us is the wild strawberry than the pineapple, the wild apple than the orange, the hazelnut or pignut than the cocoanut or almond, and not on account of their flavor merely, but the part they play in our education.

JOURNAL, November 26, 1860.

ON EDUCATION

❧ The audience are never tired of hearing how far the wind carried some man, woman, or child, or family Bible, but they are immediately tired if you undertake to give them a scientific account of it.

JOURNAL, February 4, 1852.

❧ How few ever get beyond feeding, clothing, sheltering, and warming themselves in this world, and begin to treat themselves as human beings—as intellectual and moral beings! Most seem not to see any further—and not to see over the ridge-pole of their barns—or to be exhausted and accomplish nothing more than a full barn, though it may be accompanied by an empty head. They venture a little, run some risks, when it is a question of a larger crop of corn or potatoes; but they are commonly timid and count their coppers, when the question is whether their children shall be educated. He who has the reputation of being the thriftiest farmer and making the best bargains is really the most thriftless and makes the worst. It is the safest to invest in knowledge, for the probability is that you can carry that with you wherever you go.

JOURNAL, January 3, 1861.

On Institutions   ✍   ✍

✍   How much of the life of certain men *goes* to sustain, to make respected, the institutions of society. They are the ones who pay the heaviest tax.

JOURNAL, September 6, 1851.

✍   I love man—kind, but I hate the institutions of the dead unkind. Men execute nothing so faithfully as the wills of the dead, to the last codicil and letter. *They* rule the world, and the living are but their executors.

THE WEEK, Monday.

✍   In short, as a snowdrift is formed where there is a lull in the wind, so one would say, where there is a lull of truth, an institution springs up. But the truth blows right on over it, nevertheless, and at length blows it down.

LIFE WITHOUT PRINCIPLE.

ON INSTITUTIONS

🖋 I do not value any view of the universe into which man and the institutions of man enter very largely and absorb much of the attention. Man is but the place where I stand, and the prospect hence is infinite.

JOURNAL, April 2, 1852.

🖋 Let us have institutions framed not out of our rottenness, but out of our soundness. This factitious piety is like stale gingerbread. I would like to suggest what a pack of fools and cowards we mankind are. They want me to agree not to breathe too hard in the neighborhood of their paper castles. If I should draw a long breath in the neighborhood of these institutions, their weak and flabby sides would fall out, for my own inspiration would exhaust the air about them.

JOURNAL, November 16, 1858.

🖋 I hardly know an *intellectual* man, even, who is so broad and truly liberal that you can think aloud in his society. Most with whom you endeavor to talk soon come to a stand against some institution in which they appear to hold stock—that is, some particular, not universal, way of viewing things. They will continually thrust their own low roof, with its narrow skylight, between you and the sky, when it is the unobstructed heavens you wish to view.

LIFE WITHOUT PRINCIPLE.

🖋 A temple, you know, was anciently "an open place without a roof," whose walls served merely to shut out the world and direct the mind toward heaven; but a modern *meeting-house* shuts out the heavens, while it crowds the world into still closer quarters.

LETTER TO HARRISON BLAKE, July 21, 1852.

If it were not for death and funerals, I think the institution of the Church would not stand longer.

JOURNAL, November 16, 1851.

It is surprising to what extent the world is ruled by cliques. They who constitute, or at least lead, New England or New York society, in the eyes of the world, are but a clique, a few "men of the age" and of the town, who work best in the harness provided for them. The institutions of almost all kinds are thus of a sectarian or party character. Newspapers, magazines, colleges, and all forms of government and religion express the superficial activity of a few, the mass either conforming or not attending.

JOURNAL, August 9, 1858.

The cars come and go with such regularity and precision, and the whistle and rumble are heard so far, that town clocks and family clocks are already half dispensed with, and it is easy to foresee that one extensive well-conducted and orderly institution like a railroad will keep time and order for a whole country. The startings and arrivals of the cars are the epochs in a village day.

JOURNAL, June 8, 1850.

The way in which men cling to old institutions after the life has departed out of them, and out of themselves, reminds me of those monkeys which cling by their tails—aye, whose tails contract about the limbs, even the dead limbs, of the forest, and they hang suspended beyond the hunter's reach long after they are dead. It is of no use to argue with such men. They have not the apprehensive intellect, but merely, as it were, a prehensile tail.

JOURNAL, August 19, 1851.

On Possessions ❦ ❦

❦ All good things are cheap; all bad are very dear.

JOURNAL, March 3, 1841.

❦ I am amused to see from my window here how busily man has divided and staked off his dominion. God must smile at his puny fences running hither and thither everywhere over the land.

JOURNAL, February 20, 1842.

❦ I see young men, my townsmen, whose misfortune it is to have inherited farms, houses, barns, cattle, and farming tools; for these are more easily acquired than got rid of. Better if they had been born in the open pasture and suckled by a wolf, that they might have seen with clearer eyes what field they were called to labor in. Who made them serfs of the soil? Why should they eat their sixty acres, when man is condemned to eat only his peck of dirt? Why should they begin digging their graves as soon as they are born? They have got to live a man's life, pushing all those things before them, and get on as well as they can. How many a poor immortal soul have I met well-nigh crushed and smothered under its load, creeping down the road of life, pushing before it a barn seventy-five feet by forty, its Augean stables never cleansed, and one hundred acres of land, tillage, mowing, pasture, and wood-lot! The portionless, who struggle with no such unnecessary inherited encumbrances, find it labor enough to subdue and cultivate a few cubic feet of flesh.

WALDEN, *Chapter I.*

❁ I bought me a spy-glass some weeks since. I buy but few things, and those not till long after I begin to want them, so that when I do get them I am prepared to make a perfect use of them and extract their whole sweet.

JOURNAL, April 10, 1854.

❁ If a hen puts her eggs elsewhere than in the barns —in woods or among rocks—she is said to *steal* her nest!

JOURNAL, July 16, 1851.

❁ The better part of the man is soon plowed into the soil for compost. By a seeming fate, commonly called necessity, they are employed, as it says in an old book, laying up treasures which moth and rust will corrupt and thieves break through and steal. It is a fool's life, as they will find when they get to the end of it, if not before.

WALDEN, *Chapter I.*

❁ The assessors called me into their office this year and said they wished to get an inventory of my property; asked if I had any real estate. No. Any notes at interest

or railroad shares? No. Any taxable property? None that
I knew of. "I own a boat," I said; and one of them thought
that that might come under the head of a pleasure car-
riage, which is taxable.

JOURNAL, November 30, 1855.

❦ If you mean by hard times, times, not when there is
no bread, but when there is no cake, I have no sympathy
with you.

JOURNAL, January 28, 1852.

❦ Does he chiefly own the land who coldly uses it and
gets corn and potatoes out of it, or he who loves it and
gets inspiration from it? How rarely a man's love for nature becomes a ruling principle with him, like a youth's
affection for a maiden, but more enduring! All nature is
my bride. That nature which to one is a stark and ghastly
solitude is a sweet, tender, and genial society to another.

JOURNAL, April 23, 1857.

❦ I talked of buying Conantum once, but for want of
money we did not come to terms. But I have farmed it in
my own fashion every year since.

JOURNAL, August 31, 1851.

❦ I cannot but feel compassion when I hear some trig,
compact-looking man, seemingly free, all girded and
ready, speak of his "furniture," as whether it is insured or
not. "But what shall I do with my furniture?" My gay
butterfly is entangled in a spider's web then.

WALDEN, Chapter I.

On Work 🦋 🦋

🦋 It is not enough to be industrious; so are the ants.
What are you industrious about?

> *LETTER TO HARRISON BLAKE, November 16, 1857.*

🦋 If you have built castles in the air, your work need
not be lost; that is where they should be. Now put the
foundations under them.

> *WALDEN, Chapter XVIII.*

🦋 Most men would feel insulted if it were proposed to
employ them in throwing stones over a wall, and then in
throwing them back, merely that they might earn their
wages. But many are no more worthily employed now.

> *LIFE WITHOUT PRINCIPLE.*

🦋 Nothing remarkable was ever accomplished in a
prosaic mood.

> *CAPE COD, Chapter VI.*

249

How happens it that there are few men so well employed—so much to their mind—but that a little money or fame would buy them off from their present pursuits?

JOURNAL, September 7, 1851.

The farmer is endeavoring to solve the problem of a livelihood by a formula more complicated than the problem itself. To get his shoestrings he speculates in herds of cattle. With consummate skill he has set his trap with a hair spring to catch comfort and independence, and then, as he turned away, got his own leg into it.

WALDEN, Chapter I.

I would not be one of those who will foolishly drive a nail into mere lath and plastering; such a deed would keep we awake nights. Give me a hammer, and let me feel for the furring. Do not depend on the putty. Drive a nail home and clinch it so faithfully that you can wake up in the night and think of your work with satisfaction —a work at which you would not be ashamed to invoke the Muse. So will help you God, and so only. Every nail driven should be as another rivet in the machine of the universe, you carrying on the work.

WALDEN, Chapter XVIII.

After a hard day's work without a thought, turning my very brain into a mere tool, only in the quiet of evening do I so far recover my senses as to hear the cricket, which in fact has been chirping all day.

JOURNAL, June 22, 1851.

ON WORK

It is remarkable that there is little or nothing to be remembered written on the subject of getting a living; how to make getting a living not merely honest and honorable, but altogether inviting and glorious; for if *getting* a living is not so, then living is not.

LIFE WITHOUT PRINCIPLE.

Cold and hunger seem more friendly to my nature than those methods which men have adopted and advise to ward them off.

LIFE WITHOUT PRINCIPLE.

Most men, even in this comparatively free country, through mere ignorance and mistake, are so occupied with the factitious cares and superfluously coarse labors of life that its finer fruits cannot be plucked by them.

WALDEN, Chapter I.

The weapons with which we have gained our most important victories, which should be handed down as heirlooms from father to son, are not the sword and the lance, but the bushwhack, the turf-cutter, the spade, and the bog hoe, rusted with the blood of many a meadow, and begrimed with the dust of many a hard-fought field.

WALKING.

Do not hire a man who does your work for money, but him who does it for love of it.

LIFE WITHOUT PRINCIPLE.

251

⚘ The ways by which you may get money almost without exception lead downward. To have done anything by which you earned money *merely* is to have been truly idle or worse. If the laborer gets no more than the wages which his employer pays him, he is cheated, he cheats himself.

LIFE WITHOUT PRINCIPLE.

⚘ There is a certain Irish woodchopper who, when I come across him at his work in the woods in the winter, never fails to ask me what time it is, as if he were in haste to take his dinner-pail and go home. This is not as it should be. Every man, and the woodchopper among the rest, should love his work as much as the poet does his. All good political arrangements proceed on this supposition. If labor mainly, or to any considerable degree, serves the purpose of a police, to keep men out of mischief, it indicates a rottenness at the foundation of our community.

JOURNAL, December 12, 1859.

⚘ Work your vein till it is exhausted, or conducts you to a broader one.

LETTER TO DANIEL RICKETSON, March 5, 1856.

⚘ If it were not that I desire to do something here— accomplish some work—I should certainly prefer to suffer and die rather than be at the pains to get a living by the modes men propose.

JOURNAL, February 18, 1851.

ON WORK

※ One says to me, "I wonder that you do not lay up money; you love to travel; you might take the cars and go to Fitchburg today and see the country." But I am wiser than that. I have learned that the swiftest traveler is he who goes afoot. I say to my friend, Suppose we try who will get there first. The distance is thirty miles; the fare ninety cents. That is almost a day's wages. I remember when wages were sixty cents a day for laborers on this very road. Well, I start now on foot, and get there before night; I have traveled at that rate by the week together. You will in the meanwhile have earned your fare, and arrive there some time tomorrow, or possibly this evening, if you are lucky enough to get a job in season. Instead of going to Fitchburg, you will be working here the greater part of the day.

WALDEN, *Chapter I.*

※ No amusement has worn better than farming. It tempts men just as strongly today as in the day of Cincinnatus. Healthily and properly pursued, it is not a whit more grave than huckleberrying, and if it takes any airs on itself as superior there's something wrong about it.

JOURNAL, October 29, 1857.

※ The ways in which most men get their living, that is, live, are mere makeshifts, and a shirking of the real business of life—chiefly because they do not know, but partly because they do not mean, any better.

LIFE WITHOUT PRINCIPLE.

253

I deal so much with my fuel—what with finding it, loading it, conveying it home, sawing and splitting it— get so many values out of it, am warmed in so many ways by it, that the heat it will yield when in the stove is of a lower temperature and a lesser value in my eyes— though when I feel it I am reminded of all my adventures. I just turned to put on a stick. I had my choice in the box of gray chestnut rail, black and brown snag of an oak stump, dead white pine top, gray and round, with stubs of limbs, or else old bridge plank, and chose the last. Yes, I lose sight of the ultimate uses of this wood and work, the immediate ones are so great, and yet most of mankind, those called most successful in obtaining the necessaries of life—getting their living—obtain none of this, except a mere vulgar and perhaps stupefying warmth.

JOURNAL, November 9, 1855.

I hate the present modes of living and getting a living. Farming and shopkeeping and working at a trade or profession are all odious to me. I should relish getting my living in a simple, primitive fashion. The life which society proposes to me to live is so artificial and complex —bolstered up on so many weak supports, and sure to topple down at last—that no man surely can ever be inspired to live it, and only "old fogies" ever praise it. At best some think it their duty to live it. I believe in the infinite joy and satisfaction of helping myself and others to the extent of my ability. But what is the use of trying to live simply, raising what you eat, making what you wear, building what you inhabit, burning what you cut or dig, when those to whom you are allied insanely want and will have a thousand other things which neither you nor they can raise and nobody else, perchance, will pay for? The fellow-man to whom you are yoked is a steer that is ever bolting right the other way.

JOURNAL, November 5, 1855.

🥀 Many of our days should be spent, not in vain expectations and lying on our oars, but in carrying out deliberately and faithfully the hundred little purposes which every man's genius must have suggested to him. Let not your life be wholly without an object, though it be only to ascertain the flavor of a cranberry, for it will not be only the quality of an insignificant berry that you will have tasted, but the flavor of your life to that extent, and it will be such a sauce as no wealth can buy.

JOURNAL, August 30, 1856.

🥀 For more than five years I maintained myself thus solely by the labor of my hands, and I found that, by working about six weeks in a year, I could meet all the expenses of living. The whole of my winters, as well as most of my summers, I had free and clear for study.

WALDEN, Chapter I.

On Opinion ❈ ❈

❈ Public opinion is a weak tyrant compared with private opinion. What I think of myself, that determines my fate.

JOURNAL, 1845–47.

❈ There is a stronger desire to be respectable to one's neighbors than to one's self.

JOURNAL, 1845–47.

❈ What is the value of his esteem who does not justly esteem another?

JOURNAL, February 15, 1851.

❈ They who merely have a talent for affairs are forward to express their opinions. A Roman soldier sits there to decide upon the righteousness of Christ.

JOURNAL, August 19, 1851.

❀ That nation is not Christian where the principles of humanity do not prevail, but the prejudices of race. I expect the Christian not to be superstitious, but to be distinguished by the clearness of his knowledge, the strength of his faith, the breadth of his humanity. A man of another race, an African for instance, comes to America to travel through it, and he meets with treatment exactly similar to, or worse than, that which the American meets with among the Turks, and Arabs, and Tartars.

JOURNAL, September 25, 1851.

❀ I live in an age when men have agreed to say "God" instead of "Jove."

JOURNAL, January 30, 1852.

❀ It is never too late to give up our prejudices. No way of thinking or doing, however ancient, can be trusted without proof. What everybody echoes or in silence passes by as true today may turn out to be a falsehood tomorrow, mere smoke of opinion, which some had trusted for a cloud that would sprinkle fertilizing rain on their fields. What old people say you cannot do, you try and find that you can. Old deeds for old people, and new deeds for new.

WALDEN, Chapter I.

❀ I go to see many a good man or good woman, so called, and utter freely that thought which alone it was given to me to utter; but there was a man who lived a long, long time ago, and his name was Moses, and another whose name was Christ, and if your thought does not, or does not appear to, coincide with what they said, the good man or the good woman has no ears to hear you. They think they love God! It is only his old clothes, of which they make scarecrows for the children.

JOURNAL, November 16, 1851.

We check and repress the divinity that stirs within us, to fall down and worship the divinity that is dead without us.

JOURNAL, November 16, 1851.

The amount of it is, if the majority vote the devil to be God, the minority will live and behave accordingly, and obey the successful candidate, trusting that, some time or other, by some speaker's casting-vote, perhaps, they may reinstate God. This is the highest principle I can get out or invent for my neighbors. These men act as if they believed that they could safely slide down a hill a little way—or a good way—and would surely come to a place, by and by, where they could begin to slide up again. This is expediency, or choosing that course which offers the slightest obstacles to the feet, that is, a down-hill one. But there is no such thing as accomplishing a righteous reform by the use of "expediency." There is no such thing as sliding uphill. In morals the only sliders are backsliders.

SLAVERY IN MASSACHUSETTS.

The entertaining a single thought of a certain elevation makes all men of one religion. It is always some base alloy that creates the distinction of sects.

JOURNAL, August 8, 1852.

I sometimes despair of getting anything quite simple and honest done in this world by the help of men. They would have to be passed through a powerful press first, to squeeze their old notions out of them, so that they would not soon get upon their legs again; and then there would be some one in the company with a maggot in his head, hatched from an egg deposited there nobody knows when, for not even fire kills these things, and you would have lost your labor.

WALDEN, Chapter I.

Always you have to contend with the stupidity of men. It is like a stiff soil, a hard-pan. If you go deeper than usual, you are sure to meet with a pan made harder even by the superficial cultivation. The stupid you have always with you. Men are more obedient at first to words than ideas. They mind names more than things. Read them a lecture on "Education," naming that subject, and they will think that they have heard something important, but call it "Transcendentalism," and they will think it moonshine.

JOURNAL, February 13, 1860.

All a man's strength and all his weakness go to make up the authority of any particular opinion which he may utter. He is strong or weak with all his strength and weakness combined.

JOURNAL, February 16, 1854.

�֍ As to how to preserve potatoes from rotting, your opinion may change from year to year; but as to how to preserve your soul from rotting, I have nothing to learn, but something to practice.

LETTER TO HARRISON BLAKE, February 27, 1853.

On Conservation ✠ ✠

✠ As in many countries precious metals belong to the crown, so here more precious natural objects of rare beauty should belong to the public.

JOURNAL, January 3, 1861.

✠ If some are prosecuted for abusing children, others deserve to be prosecuted for maltreating the face of nature committed to their care.

JOURNAL, September 28, 1857.

✠ The Indian stood nearer wild nature than we. The wildest and noblest quadrupeds, even the largest fresh-water fishes, some of the wildest and noblest birds and the fairest flowers have actually receded as *we* advanced, and we have but the most distant knowledge of them.

JOURNAL, March 5, 1858.

In Boston yesterday an ornithologist said significantly, "If you held the bird in your hand—"; but I would rather hold it in my affections.

JOURNAL, May 10, 1854.

When a new country like North America is discovered, a few feeble efforts are made to Christianize the natives before they are all exterminated, but they are not found to pay, in any sense. But the energetic traders of the discovering country organize themselves, or rather inevitably crystallize, into a vast rat-catching society, tempt the natives to become mere vermin-hunters and rum-drinkers, reserving half a continent for the field of their labors. Savage meets savage, and the white man's only distinction is that he is the chief.

JOURNAL, April 8, 1859.

We cut down the few old oaks which witnessed the transfer of the township from the Indian to the white man, and commence our museum with a cartridge-box taken from a British soldier in 1775!

JOURNAL, January 3, 1861.

It is a thorough process, this war with the wilderness —breaking nature, taming the soil, feeding it on oats. The civilized man regards the pine tree as his enemy. He will fell it and let in the light, grub it up and raise wheat or rye there. It is no better than a fungus to him.

JOURNAL, February 2, 1852.

⚘ Each town should have a park, or rather a primitive forest, of five hundred or a thousand acres, where a stick should never be cut for fuel, a common possession forever, for instruction and recreation. We hear of cow-commons and ministerial lots, but we want *men*-commons and lay lots, inalienable forever. Let us keep the New World *new*, preserve all the advantages of living in the country. There is meadow and pasture and wood-lot for the town's poor. Why not a forest and huckleberry-field for the town's rich? All Walden Wood might have been preserved for our park forever, with Walden in its midst, and the Esterbrooks Country, an unoccupied area of some four square miles, might have been our huckleberry-field.

JOURNAL, October 15, 1859.

⚘ As some give to Harvard College or another institution, why might not another give a forest or huckleberry-field to Concord? A town is an institution which deserves to be remembered. We boast of our system of education, but why stop at schoolmasters and schoolhouses? We are all schoolmasters, and our schoolhouse is the universe. To attend chiefly to the desk or schoolhouse while we neglect the scenery in which it is placed is absurd. If we do not look out we shall find our fine schoolhouse standing in a cow-yard at last.

JOURNAL, October 15, 1859.

⚘ What is the use of a house if you haven't got a tolerable planet to put it on?

LETTER TO HARRISON BLAKE, May 20, 1860.

❈ I spent a considerable portion of my time observing the habits of the wild animals, my brute neighbors. By their various movements and migrations they fetch the year about to me. Very significant are the flight of geese and the migration of suckers, etc., etc. But when I consider that the nobler animals have been exterminated here—the cougar, panther, lynx, wolverine, wolf, bear, moose, deer, the beaver, the turkey, etc., etc.,—I cannot but feel as if I lived in a tamed, and, as it were, emasculated country. Would not the motions of those larger and wilder animals have been more significant still? Is it not a maimed and imperfect nature that I am conversant with? As if I were to study a tribe of Indians that had lost all its warriors.

JOURNAL, March 23, 1856.

❈ We seem to think that the earth must go through the ordeal of sheep-pasturage before it is habitable by man.

THE MAINE WOODS, Chesuncook.

❈ Think of a mountain-top in the township—even to the minds of the Indians a sacred place—only accessible through private grounds! A temple, as it were, which you cannot enter except by trespassing and at the risk of letting out or letting in somebody's cattle! In fact, the temple itself in this case private property and standing in a man's cow-yard—for such is commonly the case!

JOURNAL, January 3, 1861.

ON CONSERVATION

⚔ New Hampshire courts have lately been deciding—as if it was for them to decide—whether the top of Mt. Washington belonged to A or to B; and, it being decided in favor of B, as I hear, he went up one winter with the proper officer and took formal possession of it. But I think that the top of Mt. Washington should not be private property; it should be left unappropriated for modesty and reverence's sake, or if only to suggest that earth has higher uses than we put her to.

JOURNAL, January 3, 1861.

⚔ It would be worth the while if in each town there were a committee appointed to see that the beauty of the town received no detriment. If we have the largest boulder in the county, then it should not belong to an individual, nor be made into door-steps.

JOURNAL, January 3, 1861.

⚔ The catechism says that the chief end of man is to glorify God and enjoy him forever, which of course is applicable mainly to God as seen in his works. Yet the only account of its beautiful insects—butterflies, etc.—which God has made and set before us which the State ever thinks of spending any money on is the account of those which are injurious to vegetation! This is the way we glorify God and enjoy him forever. Come out here and behold a thousand painted butterflies and other beautiful insects which people the air, then go to the libraries and see what kind of prayer and glorification of God is there recorded. Massachusetts has published her report on "Insects Injurious to Vegetation," and our neighbor the "Noxious Insects of New York."

JOURNAL, May 1, 1859.

🦋 Children are attracted by the beauty of butterflies, but their parents and legislators deem it an idle pursuit. The parents remind me of the devil, but the children of God. Though God may have pronounced his work good, we ask, "Is it not poisonous?"

JOURNAL, May 1, 1859.

🦋 It is remarkable that many men will go with eagerness to Walden Pond in the winter to fish for pickerel and yet not seem to care for the landscape. Of course it cannot be *merely* for the pickerel they may catch; there is some adventure in it; but any love of nature which they may feel is certainly very slight and indefinite. They call it going a-fishing, and so indeed it is, though, perchance, their natures know better. Now I go a-fishing and a-hunting every day, but omit the fish and the game, which are the least important part. I have learned to do without them. They were indispensable only as long as I was a boy.

JOURNAL, January 26, 1853.

🦋 Most men, it seems to me, do not care for Nature and would sell their share in all her beauty, as long as they may live, for a stated sum—many for a glass of rum. Thank God, men cannot as yet fly, and lay waste the sky as well as the earth!

JOURNAL, January 3, 1861.

ON CONSERVATION

🌿 Whatever a great many grown-up boys are seriously engaged in is considered great and good, and, as such, is sure of the recognition of the churchman and statesman. What, for instance, are the blue juniper berries in the pasture, which the cowboy remembers so far as they are beautiful merely, to church or state? Mere trifles which deserve and get no protection. As an object of beauty, though significant to all who really live in the country, they do not receive the protection of any community. Anybody may grub up all that exist.

JOURNAL, November 28, 1860.

🌿 I fear that he who walks over these fields a century hence will not know the pleasure of knocking off wild apples. Ah, poor man, there are many pleasures which he will not know!

WILD APPLES.

🌿 Some thoughtless and cruel sportsman has killed twenty-two young partridges not much bigger than robins, against the laws of Massachusetts and humanity.

JOURNAL, July 16, 1851.

🌿 The smokes from a dozen clearings far and wide, from a portion of the earth thirty miles or more in diameter, reveal the employment of many husbandmen at this season. Thus I see the woods burned up from year to year. The telltale smokes reveal it. The smokes will become rarer and thinner year by year, till I shall detect only a mere feathery film and there is no more brush to be burned.

JOURNAL, October 10, 1857.

By avarice and selfishness, and a groveling habit, from which none of us is free, of regarding the soil as property, or the means of acquiring property chiefly, the landscape is deformed, husbandry is degraded with us, and the farmer leads the meanest of lives. He knows Nature but as a robber.

WALDEN, Chapter VII.

The very willow-rows lopped every three years for fuel or powder, and every sizable pine or oak, or other forest tree, cut down within the memory of man! As if individual speculators were to be allowed to export the clouds out of the sky, or the stars out of the firmament, one by one. We shall be reduced to gnaw the very crust of the earth for nutriment.

THE MAINE WOODS, Chesuncook.

The Anglo-American can indeed cut down, and grub up all this waving forest, and make a stump speech, and vote for Buchanan on its ruins, but he cannot converse with the spirit of the tree he fells, he cannot read the poetry and mythology which retire as he advances. He ignorantly erases mythological tablets in order to print his handbills and town-meeting warrants on them.

THE MAINE WOODS, Allegash.

Strange that so few ever come to the woods to see how the pine tree lives and grows and spires, lifting its evergreen arms to the light—to see its perfect success; but most are content to behold it in the shape of many broad boards brought to market, and deem *that* its true success! But the pine is no more lumber than man is, and to be made into boards and houses is no more its true and highest use than the truest use of a man is to be cut down and made into manure. There is a higher law affecting our relation to pines as well as to men. A pine cut down, a dead pine, is no more a pine than a dead carcass is a man. Can he who has discovered only some of the values of whalebone and whale oil be said to have discovered the true use of the whale? Can he who slays the elephant for his ivory be said to have "seen the elephant?" These are petty and accidental uses; just as if a stronger race were to kill us in order to make buttons and flageolets of our bones; for everything may serve a lower as well as a higher use. Every creature is better alive than dead, men and moose and pine trees, and he who understands it aright will rather preserve its life than destroy it.

THE MAINE WOODS, Chesuncook.

When the chopper would praise a pine, he will commonly tell you that the one he cut was so big that a yoke of oxen stood on its stump; as if that were what the pine had grown for, to become the footstool of oxen.

THE MAINE WOODS, Allegash.

The explorers and lumberers generally are all hirelings, paid so much a day for their labor, and as such they have no more love for wild nature than wood-sawyers have for forests. Other white men and Indians who come here are for the most part hunters, whose object it is to slay as many moose and other wild animals as possible. But, pray, could not one spend some weeks or years in

the solitude of this vast wilderness with other employments than these—employments perfectly sweet and innocent and ennobling? For one that comes with a pencil
to sketch or sing, a thousand come with an axe or rifle.

THE MAINE WOODS, Chesuncook.

I thought with regret how soon these trees, like the
black birches that grew on the hill nearby, would be all
cut off, and there would be almost nothing of the old
Concord left, and we should be reduced to read old deeds
in order to be reminded of such things—deeds, at least,
in which some old and revered bound trees are mentioned.
These will be the only proof at last that they ever existed.
Pray, farmers, keep some old woods to match the old deeds.
Keep them for history's sake, as specimens of what the
township was. Let us not be reduced to a mere paper
evidence, to deeds kept in a chest or secretary, when not
so much as the bark of the paper birch will be left for
evidence, about its decayed stump.

JOURNAL, November 8, 1858.

What are the natural features which make a township handsome? A river, with its waterfalls and meadows,
a lake, a hill, a cliff or individual rocks, a forest, and
ancient trees standing singly. Such things are beautiful;
they have a high use which dollars and cents never represent. If the inhabitants of a town were wise, they would
seek to preserve these things, though at a considerable
expense; for such things educate far more than any hired
teachers or preachers, or any at present recognized system

of school education. I do not think him fit to be the founder of a state or even of a town who does not foresee the use of these things, but legislates chiefly for oxen, as it were.

JOURNAL, *January 3, 1861.*

※ We accuse the savages of worshipping only the bad spirit, or devil, though they may distinguish both a good and a bad; but they regard only that one which they fear and worship the devil only. We, too, are savages in this, doing precisely the same thing. This occurred to me yesterday as I sat in the woods admiring the beauty of a blue butterfly. We are not chiefly interested in birds and insects, for example, as they are ornamental to the earth and cheering to man, but we spare the life of the former only on condition that they eat more grubs than cherries, and the only account of the insects in which the State encourages is of the "Insects *Injurious* to Vegetation."

JOURNAL, *May 1, 1859.*

※ Respecting lichens, perhaps the first question which the mass of men put is, "What ones are good to eat?"

JOURNAL, *February 9, 1852.*

※ I cannot but see still in my mind's eye those little striped breams poised in Walden's glaucous water. They balance all the rest of the world in my estimation at present, for this is the bream that I have just found, and for the time I neglect all its brethren and am ready to kill the fatted calf on its account. For more than two centuries men have fished here and have not distinguished this permanent settler of the township. It is not like a new bird, a transient visitor that may not be seen again for years, but there it dwells and has dwelt permanently, who can tell how long? But in my account of this bream I cannot go a hair's breadth beyond the mere statement that it exists—the miracle of its existence, my contemporary and neighbor, yet so different from me! I can only poise my thought there by its side and try to think like a bream for a moment. I only see the bream in its orbit, as I see a star, but I care not to measure its distance or weight. The bream, appreciated, floats in the pond as the center of the system, another image of God. Its life no man can explain more than he can his own. I have a contemporary in Walden. It has fins where I have legs and arms. I have a friend among the fishes, at least a new acquaintance. Its character will interest me, I trust, not its clothes and anatomy. I do not want it to eat.

JOURNAL, November 30, 1858.

When the question of the protection of birds comes up, the legislatures regard only a low use and never a high use; the best-disposed legislators employ one, perchance, only to examine their crops and see how many grubs or cherries they contain, and never to study their dispositions, or the beauty of their plumage, or listen and report on the sweetness of their song. The legislature will preserve a bird professedly not because it is a beautiful creature, but because it is a good scavenger or the like. This, at least, is the defense set up. It is as if the question were whether some celebrated singer of the human race—some Jenny Lind or another—did more harm or good, should be destroyed, or not, and therefore a committee should be appointed, not to listen to her singing at all, but to examine the contents of her stomach and see if she devoured anything which was injurious to the farmers and gardeners, or which they cannot spare.

JOURNAL, April 8, 1859.

I would rather save one of these hawks than have a hundred hens and chickens. It is worth more to see them soar, especially now that they are so rare in the landscape. It is easy to buy eggs, but not to buy hen-hawks. My neighbors would not hesitate to shoot the last pair of hen-hawks in the town to save a few of their chickens! But such economy is narrow and grovelling. It is unnecessarily to sacrifice the greater value to the less. I would rather never taste chickens' meat nor hens' eggs than never to see a hawk sailing through the upper air again. This sight is worth incomparably more than a chicken soup or a boiled egg. So we exterminate the deer and substitute the hog.

JOURNAL, June 13, 1853.

In my boating of late I have several times scared up a couple of summer ducks of this year, bred in our meadows. They allowed me to come quite near, and helped to people the river. I have not seen them for some days. Would you know the end of our intercourse? Goodwin shot them, and Mrs. ——, who never sailed on the river, ate them. Of course, she knows not what she did. What if I should eat her canary? Thus we share each other's sins as well as burdens. The lady who watches admiringly the matador shares his deed. They belonged to me, as much as to anyone, when they were alive, but it was considered of more importance that Mrs. —— should taste the flavor of them dead than that I should enjoy the beauty of them alive.

JOURNAL, August 16, 1858.

What a pitiful business is the fur trade, which has been pursued now for so many ages, for so many years by famous companies which enjoy a profitable monopoly and control a large portion of the earth's surface, unweariedly pursuing and ferreting out small animals by the aid of all the loafing class tempted by rum and money, that you may rob some little fellow-creature of its coat to adorn or thicken your own, that you may get a fashionable covering in which to hide your head, or a suitable robe in which to dispense justice to your fellow-men! Regarded from the philosopher's point of view, it is precisely on a level with rag and bone picking in the streets of the cities. Think how many musquash and weasel skins the Hudson's Bay Company pile up annually in their warehouses, leaving the bare red carcasses on the banks of streams throughout all British America—and this it is, chiefly, which makes it *British* America. It is the place where Great Britain goes a-mousing. We have heard much of the wonderful intelligence of the beaver, but that regard for the beaver is all a pretense, and we would give more for a beaver hat than to preserve the intelligence of the whole race of beavers.

JOURNAL, April 8, 1859.

ON CONSERVATION

🗶 We will fine Abner if he shoots a singing bird, but encourage the army of Abners that compose the Hudson's Bay Company.

JOURNAL, April 8, 1859.

🗶 But this hunting of the moose merely for the satisfaction of killing him—not even for the sake of his hide—without making any extraordinary exertion or running any risk yourself, is too much like going out by night to some wood-side pasture and shooting your neighbor's horses. These are God's own horses, poor, timid creatures, that will run fast enough as soon as they smell you, though they *are* nine feet high. Joe told us of some hunters who a year or two before had shot down several oxen by night, somewhere in the Maine woods, mistaking them for moose. And so might any of the hunters; and what is the difference in the sport, but the name? In the former case, having killed one of God's and *your own* oxen, you strip off its hide—because that is the common trophy, and, moreover, you have heard that it may be sold for moccasins—cut a steak from its haunches, and leave the huge carcass to smell to heaven for you. It is no better, at least, than to assist at a slaughter-house.

THE MAINE WOODS, Chesuncook.

🗶 In some countries a hunting parson is no uncommon sight. Such a one might make a good shepherd's dog, but is far from being the Good Shepherd.

WALDEN, Chapter XI.

275

⚜ Yet what is the character of our gratitude to these squirrels, these planters of forests? We regard them as vermin, and annually shoot and destroy them in great numbers, because—if we have any excuse—they sometimes devour a little of our Indian corn, while, perhaps, they are planting the nobler oak-corn (acorn) in its place. In various parts of the country an army of grown-up boys assembles for a squirrel hunt. They choose sides, and the side that kills the greatest number of thousands enjoys a supper at the expense of the other side, and the whole neighborhood rejoices. Would it not be far more civilized and humane, not to say godlike, to recognize once in the year by some significant symbolical ceremony the part which the squirrel plays, the great service it performs, in the economy of the universe?

JOURNAL, October 22, 1860.

⚜ Primitive Nature is the most interesting to me. I take infinite pains to know all the phenomena of the spring, for instance, thinking that I have here the entire poem, and then, to my chagrin, I hear that it is but an imperfect copy that I possess and have read, that my ancestors have torn out many of the first leaves and grandest passages, and mutilated it in many places. I should not like to think that some demigod have come before me and picked out some of the best of the stars. I wish to know an entire heaven and an entire earth.

JOURNAL, March 23, 1856.

⚜ When you get to Europe you will meet the most tender-hearted and delicately bred lady, perhaps the President of the Antislavery Society, or of that for the encouragement of humanity to animals, marching or presiding with the scales from a tortoise's back—obtained by laying live coals on it to make them curl up—stuck in her hair, rat-skin fitting as close to her fingers as erst to the rat, and, for her cloak, trimmings perchance adorned with the spoils of a hundred skunks—rendered inodorous, we trust. Poor misguided woman! Could she not wear other armor in the war of humanity?

JOURNAL, April 8, 1859.

Why should not we, who have renounced the king's authority, have our national preserves, where no villages need be destroyed, in which the bear and panther, and some even of the hunter race, may still exist, and not be "civilized off the face of the earth"—our forests, not to hold the king's game merely, but to hold and preserve the king himself also, the lord of creation—not for idle sport or food, but for inspiration, and our own true recreation? Or shall we, like the villains, grub them all up, poaching on our national domains?

THE MAINE WOODS, Chesuncook.

In old countries, as England, going across lots is out of the question. You must walk in some beaten path or other, though it may be a narrow one. We are tending to the same state of things here, when practically a few will have grounds of their own, but most will have none to walk over but what the few allow them.

JOURNAL, January 3, 1861.

At present, in this vicinity, the best part of the land is not private property; the landscape is not owned, and the walker enjoys comparative freedom. But possibly the day will come when it will be partitioned off into so-called pleasure-grounds, in which a few will take a narrow and exclusive pleasure only—when fences shall be multiplied, and man-traps and other engines invented to confine men to the *public* road, and walking over the surface of God's earth shall be construed to mean trespassing on some gentleman's grounds. To enjoy a thing exclusively is commonly to exclude yourself from the true enjoyment of it. Let us improve our opportunities, then, before the evil days come.

WALKING.

On Courage ✳ ✳

✳ A man sits as many risks as he runs.
WALDEN, Chapter VI.

✳ Nothing is so much to be feared as fear.
JOURNAL, September 7, 1851.

✳ You are expected to do your duty, not in spite of every thing but *one,* but in spite of *everything.*
JOURNAL, September 24, 1859.

✳ The monster is never just there where we think he is. What is truly monstrous is our cowardice and sloth.
LETTER TO HARRISON BLAKE, December 19, 1854.

✳ If a man were to place himself in an attitude to bear manfully the greatest evil that can be inflicted on him, he would find suddenly that there was no such evil to bear; his brave back would go a-begging.
LETTER TO HARRISON BLAKE, December 19, 1854.

✻ Whatever your sex or position, life is a battle in which you are to show your pluck, and woe be to the coward. Whether passed on a bed of sickness or a tented field, it is ever the same fair play and admits no foolish distinction. Despair and postponement are cowardice and defeat. Men were born to succeed, not to fail.

JOURNAL, March 21, 1853.

✻ In the morning we do not believe in expediency; we will start afresh, and have no patching, no temporary fixtures. The afternoon man has an interest in the past; his eye is divided, and he sees indifferently well either way.

JOURNAL, April 4, 1839.

✻ He who receives an injury is an accomplice of the wrong-doer.

JOURNAL, July 9, 1840.

✻ In the long run men hit only what they aim at. Therefore, though they should fail immediately, they had better aim at something high.

WALDEN, Chapter I.

✻ What poor crack-brains we are! Easily upset and unable to take care of ourselves! If there were a precipice at our doors, some would be found jumping off today for fear that, if they survived, they might jump off tomorrow.

JOURNAL, September 30, 1857.

✻ There is one obligation, and that is the obligation to obey the highest dictate.

JOURNAL, September 2, 1841.

ON COURAGE

❈ Most things are strong in one direction, a straw longitudinally, a board in the direction of its edge, but the brave man is a perfect sphere, which cannot fall on its flat side and is equally strong every way.

THE SERVICE.

❈ Not to grieve long for any action, but to go immediately and do freshly and otherwise, subtracts so much from the wrong.

JOURNAL, January 9, 1842.

❈ Men die of fright and live of confidence.

JOURNAL, 1850.

❈ It is the sentiment of fear and slavery and habit which makes a heathenish idolatry. Such idolaters abound in all countries, and heathen cross the seas to reform heathen, dead to bury the dead, and all go down to the pit together.

JOURNAL, August 30, 1856.

❈ A living dog is better than a dead lion. Shall a man go and hang himself because he belongs to the race of pigmies, and not be the biggest pigmy that he can? Let every one mind his own business, and endeavor to be what he was made.

WALDEN, Chapter XVIII.

❈ No people ever lived by cursing their fathers, however great a curse their fathers might have been to them.

CAPE COD, Chapter II.

❈ Fear creates danger, and courage dispels it.

JOURNAL, November 12, 1859.

On Life and Death ✍ ✍

✍ We live but a fraction of our life.

JOURNAL, June 13, 1851.

✍ The mass of men lead lives of quiet desperation. What is called resignation is confirmed desperation.

WALDEN, Chapter 1.

✍ Art is as long as ever, but life is more interrupted and less available for a man's proper pursuits.

JOURNAL, June 16, 1854.

✍ The youth gets together his materials to build a bridge to the moon, or perchance a palace or temple on the earth, and at length the middle-aged man concludes to build a woodshed with them.

JOURNAL, July 14, 1852.

ON LIFE AND DEATH

✍ My life will wait for nobody, but is being matured still irresistibly while I go about the streets and chaffer with this man and that to secure it a living. It will cut its own channel, like the mountain stream, which by the longest ridges and by level prairies is not kept from the sea finally. So flows a man's life, and will reach the sea water, if not by an earthy channel, yet in dew and rain, overleaping all barriers, with rainbows to announce its victory. It can wind as cunningly and unerringly as water that seeks its level; and shall I complain if the gods make it meander? This staying to buy me a farm is as if the Mississippi should stop to chaffer with a clamshell.

JOURNAL, April 7, 1841.

✍ The world is a cow that is hard to milk—life does not come so easy—and oh, how thinly it is watered ere we get it!

LETTER TO RALPH W. EMERSON, November 14, 1847.

✍ How meanly and miserably we live for the most part! We escape fate continually by the skin of our teeth, as the saying is. We are practically desperate. But as every man, in respect to material wealth, aims to become independent or wealthy, so, in respect to our spirits and imagination, we should have some spare capital and superfluous vigor, have some margin and leeway in which to move. What kind of gift is life unless we have spirits to enjoy it and taste its true flavor; if, in respect to spirits, we are to be forever cramped and in debt? We should first of all be full of vigor like a strong horse, and beside have the free and adventurous spirit of his driver; i.e., we should have such a reserve of elasticity and strength that we may at any time be able to put ourselves at the top of our speed and go beyond our ordinary limits, just as the invalid hires a horse. Have the gods sent us into this world —to this *muster*—to do chores, hold horses, and the like, and not given us any spending money?

JOURNAL, August 10, 1857.

I had this advantage, at least, in my mode of life, over those who were obliged to look abroad for amusement, to society and the theater, that my life itself was become my amusement, and never ceased to be novel. It was a drama of many scenes and without an end.

WALDEN, Chapter IV.

This life is not for complaint, but for satisfaction.

LETTER TO DANIEL RICKETSON, November 4, 1860.

A man has his price at the South, is worth so many dollars, and so he has at the North. Many a man here sets out by saying, I will make so many dollars by such a time, or before I die, and that is his price, as much as if he were knocked off for it by a Southern auctioneer.

JOURNAL, November 29, 1860.

The simplest and most lumpish fungus has a peculiar interest to us, compared with a mere mass of earth, because it is so obviously organic and related to ourselves, however mute. It is the expression of an idea; growth

284

according to a law; matter not dormant, not raw, but inspired, appropriated by spirit. If I take up a handful of
earth, however separately interesting the particles may
be, their relation to one another appears to be that of
mere juxtaposition generally. I might have thrown them
together thus. But the humblest fungus betrays a life akin
to my own. It is a successful poem in its kind. There is
suggested something superior to any particle of matter,
in the idea or mind which uses and arranges the particles.

JOURNAL, October 10, 1858.

There are infinite degrees of life, from that which
is next to sleep and death, to that which is forever awake
and immortal. We must not confound man and man. We
cannot conceive of a greater difference than between the
life of one man and that of another.

JOURNAL, January 13, 1857.

When we are unhurried and wise, we perceive that
only great and worthy things have any permanent and
absolute existence, that petty fears and petty pleasures
are but the shadow of the reality. This is always exhilarat-
ing and sublime. By closing the eyes and slumbering, and
consenting to be deceived by shows, men establish and
conform their daily life of routine and habit everywhere,
which still is built on purely illusory foundations. Children, who play life, discern its true law and relations more
clearly than men, who fail to live it worthily, but who
think that they are wiser by experience, that is, by failure.

WALDEN, Chapter II.

🖋 The other day I opened a muskrat's house. It was made of weeds, five feet broad at the base, and three feet high, and far and low within it was a little cavity, only a foot in diameter, where the rat dwelt. It may seem trivial, this piling up of weeds, but so the race of muskrats is preserved. We must heap up a great pile of doing, for a small diameter of being.

LETTER TO HARRISON BLAKE, December 19, 1853.

🖋 We who walk the streets and hold time together, are but the refuse of ourselves, and that life is for the shells of us—of our body and our mind—for our scurf—a thoroughly *scurvy* life. It is coffee made of coffee-grounds the twentieth time, which was only coffee the first time— while the living water leaps and sparkles by our doors.

LETTER TO HARRISON BLAKE, May 28, 1850.

🖋 I have lived some thirty years on this planet, and I have yet to hear the first syllable of valuable or even earnest advice from my seniors. They have told me nothing, and probably cannot tell me anything to the purpose. Here is life, an experiment to a great extent untried by me; but it does not avail me that they have tried it. If I have any experience which I think valuable, I am sure to reflect that this my Mentors said nothing about.

WALDEN, Chapter I.

🖋 He is the true artist whose life is his material; every stroke of the chisel must enter his own flesh and bone and not grate dully on marble.

JOURNAL, June 23, 1840.

🖎 This, our respectable daily life, on which the man of common sense, the Englishman of the world, stands so squarely, and on which our institutions are founded, is in fact the veriest illusion, and will vanish like the baseless fabric of a vision; but that faint glimmer of reality which sometimes illuminates the darkness of daylight for all men, reveals something more solid and enduring than adamant, which is in fact the cornerstone of the world.

LETTER TO HARRISON BLAKE, March 27, 1848.

🖎 How can any good depart? It does not go and come, but we.

JOURNAL, February 20, 1842.

🖎 One moment of serene and confident life is more glorious than a whole campaign of daring. We should be ready for all issues, not daring to die but daring to live.

JOURNAL, December, 1839.

🖎 There are as many strata at different levels of life as there are leaves in a book. Most men probably have lived in two or three. When on the higher levels we can remember the lower levels, but when on the lower we cannot remember the higher.

JOURNAL, June, 1850.

🖎 I have met with some barren accomplished gentlemen who seemed to have been to school all their lives and never had a vacation to live in. Oh, if they could only have been stolen by the Gypsies, and carried far beyond the reach of their guardians! They had better died in infancy and been buried under the leaves, their lips be-smeared with blackberries, and Cock Robin for their sexton.

JOURNAL, October 20, 1855.

🖋 Pursue, keep up with, circle round and round your life, as a dog does his master's chaise. Do what you love. Know your own bone; gnaw at it, bury it, unearth it, and gnaw it still.

LETTER TO HARRISON BLAKE, March 27, 1848.

🖋 The life which men praise and regard as successful is but one kind. Why should we exaggerate any one kind at the expense of the others?

WALDEN, Chapter I.

🖋 I hear a good many pretend that they are going to die; or that they have died, for aught that I know. Nonsense! I'll defy them to do it. They haven't got life enough in them. They'll deliquesce like fungi, and keep a hundred eulogists mopping the spot where they left off. Only half a dozen or so have died since the world began.

PLEA FOR CAPTAIN JOHN BROWN.

🖋 Our life should be so active and progressive as to be a journey.

JOURNAL, January 28, 1852.

🖋 It is essential that a man confine himself to pursuits —a scholar, for instance, to studies—which lie next to and conduce to his life, which do not go against the grain, either of his will or his imagination. The scholar finds in his experience some studies to be most fertile and radiant with light, others dry, barren, and dark. If he is wise, he will not persevere in the last, as a plant in a cellar will strive toward the light. He will confine the observations of his mind as closely as possible to the experience or life of his senses.

JOURNAL, March 12, 1853.

✍ "Yes, we have done great deeds, and sung divine songs, which shall never die"—that is, as long as *we* can remember them. The learned societies and the great men of Assyria—where are they? What youthful philosophers and experimentalists we are! There is not one of my readers who has yet lived a whole human life.

WALDEN, Chapter XVIII.

✍ The life in us is like the water in the river. It may rise this year higher than man has ever known it, and flood the parched uplands; even this may be the eventful year, which will drown out all our muskrats.

WALDEN, Chapter XVIII.

✍ This life we live is a strange dream, and I don't believe at all any account men give of it.

LETTER TO HIS MOTHER, August 6, 1843.

✍ That which properly constitutes the life of every man is a profound secret. Yet this is what every one would give most to know, but is himself most backward to impart.

JOURNAL, March 14, 1838.

It is a record of the mellow and ripe moments that I would keep. I would not preserve the husk of life, but the kernel.

JOURNAL, December 23, 1851.

The art of life, of a poet's life, is, not having anything to do, to do something.

JOURNAL, April 29, 1852.

In proportion as our inward life fails, we go more constantly and desperately to the post-office. You may depend upon it, that the poor fellow who walks away with the greatest number of letters, proud of his extensive correspondence, has not heard from himself this long while.

LIFE WITHOUT PRINCIPLE.

Some men endeavor to live a constrained life, to subject their whole lives to their wills, as he who said he would give a sign if he were conscious after his head was cut off—but he gave no sign. Dwell as near as possible to the channel in which your life flows.

JOURNAL, March 12, 1853.

Above all, we cannot afford not to live in the present. He is blessed over all mortals who loses no moment of the passing life in remembering the past. Unless our philosophy hears the cock crow in every barnyard within our horizon, it is belated.

WALKING.

🖊 We avoid all the calamities that may occur in a lower sphere by abiding perpetually in a higher.

JOURNAL, April 27, 1854.

🖊 I am not afraid that I will exaggerate the value and significance of life, but that I shall not be up to the occasion which it is. I shall be sorry to remember that I was there, but noticed nothing remarkable—not so much as a prince in disguise; lived in the golden age as a hired man; visited Olympus even, but fell asleep after dinner, and did not hear the conversation of the gods.

LETTER TO HARRISON BLAKE, April 3, 1850.

🖊 All our life, i.e. the living part of it, is a persistent dreaming awake. The boy does not camp in his father's yard. That would not be adventurous enough, there are too many sights and sounds to disturb the illusion; so he marches off twenty or thirty miles and there pitches his tent, where stranger inhabitants are tamely sleeping in their beds just like his father at home, and camps in *their* yard, perchance. But then he dreams uninterruptedly that he is anywhere but where he is.

JOURNAL, August 27, 1859.

🖊 I stand in awe of my body, this matter to which I am bound has become so strange to me. I fear not spirits, ghosts, of which I am one—*that* my body might—but I fear bodies. I tremble to meet them. What is this Titan that has possession of me? Talk of mysteries! Think of our life in nature—daily to be shown matter, to come in contact with it—rocks, trees, wind on our cheeks! The

solid earth! the *actual* world! the *common sense!* Con-
tact! Contact! Who are we? *Where* are we?

THE MAINE WOODS, Ktaadn.

✍ I will not plant beans and corn with so much industry another summer, but such seeds, if the seed is not lost,
as sincerity, truth, simplicity, faith, innocence, and the
like, and see if they will not grow in this soil, even with
less toil and manurance, and sustain me, for surely it has
not been exhausted for these crops. Alas! I said this to
myself; but now another summer is gone, and another,
and another, and I am obliged to say to you, Reader, that
the seeds which I planted, if indeed they *were* the seeds
of those virtues, were wormeaten or had lost their vitality,
and so did not come up.

WALDEN, Chapter VII.

✍ The millions are awake enough for physical labor;
but only one in a million is awake enough for effective
intellectual exertion, only one in a hundred million to a
poetic or divine life. To be awake is to be alive. I have
never yet met a man who was quite awake.

WALDEN, Chapter II.

✍ Ninety-nine one-hundredths of our lives we are mere
hedgers and ditchers, but from time to time we meet with
reminders of our destiny.

JOURNAL, January 13, 1857.

✍ I left the woods for as good a reason as I went there.
Perhaps it seemed to me that I had several more lives to
live, and could not spare any more time for that one.

WALDEN, Chapter XVIII.

🖋 We begin to die not in our senses or extremities, but in our divine faculties.

JOURNAL, January 27, 1854.

🖋 As one year passes into another through the medium of winter, so does this our life pass into another through the medium of death.

JOURNAL, September 8, 1851.

🖋 Dr. Bartlett handed me a paper today, desiring me to subscribe for a statue to Horace Mann. I declined, and said that I thought a man ought not any more to take up room in the world after he was dead. It is very offensive to my imagination to see the dying stiffen into statues at this rate. We should wait till their bones begin to crumble—and then avoid too near a likeness to the living.

JOURNAL, September 18, 1859.

🖋 The sad memory of departed friends is soon encrusted over with sublime and pleasing thoughts, as their monuments are overgrown with moss.

JOURNAL, March 13, 1842.

🖋 I *suppose* that I have not many months to live; but, of course, I know nothing about it. I may add that I am enjoying existence as much as ever, and regret nothing.

THOREAU'S LAST LETTER. TO MYRON B. BENTON, March 21, 1862.

On Truth ❧ ❧

❧ Rather than love, than money, than fame, give me ____ truth.

WALDEN, Chapter XVIII.

❧ I prefer the natural sky to an opium-eater's heaven.

JOURNAL, September, 1850.

❧ No face which we can give to a matter will stead us so well at last as the truth. This alone wears well. For the most part, we are not where we are, but in a false position. Through an infirmity of our natures, we suppose a case, and put ourselves into it, and hence are in two cases at the same time, and it is doubly difficult to get out. In sane moments we regard only the facts, the case that is. Say what you have to say, not what you ought. Any truth is better than make-believe.

WALDEN, Chapter XVIII.

🎖 Let us make distinctions, call things by the right names.

JOURNAL, November 28, 1860.

🎖 Some circumstantial evidence is very strong, as when you find a trout in the milk.

JOURNAL, November 11, 1850.

🎖 Men esteem truth remote, in the outskirts of the system, behind the farthest star, before Adam and after the last man. In eternity there is indeed something true and sublime. But all these times and places and occasions are now and here. God himself culminates in the present moment, and will never be more divine in the lapse of all the ages.

WALDEN, Chapter II.

🎖 Nothing is so sure to make itself known as the truth, for what else waits to be known?

JOURNAL, December 12, 1851.

🎖 They who know of no purer sources of truth, who have traced up its stream no higher, stand, and wisely stand, by the Bible and the Constitution, and drink at it there with reverence and humility; but they who behold where it comes trickling into this lake or that pool, gird up their loins once more, and continue their pilgrimage toward its fountain-head.

CIVIL DISOBEDIENCE.

🎖 I love to weigh, to settle, to gravitate toward that which most strongly and rightfully attracts me—not hang by the beam of the scale and try to weigh less—not suppose a case, but take the case that is; to travel the only path I can, and that on which no power can resist me.

WALDEN, Chapter XVIII.

A lawyer's truth is not Truth, but consistency or a consistent expediency.

CIVIL DISOBEDIENCE.

Do not seek expressions, seek thoughts to be expressed. By perseverance you get two views of the same rare truth.

JOURNAL, December 25, 1851.

I ordinarily plod along a sort of whitewashed prison entry, subject to some indifferent or even grovelling mood. I do not distinctly realize my destiny. I have turned down my light to the merest glimmer and am doing some task which I have set myself. I take incredibly narrow views, live on the limits, and have no recollection of absolute truth. Mushroom institutions hedge me in. But suddenly, in some fortunate moment, the voice of eternal wisdom reaches me, even in the strain of the sparrow, and liberates me, whets and clarifies my senses, makes me a competent witness.

JOURNAL, May 12, 1857.

Let us not underrate the value of a fact; it will one day flower in a truth.

NATURAL HISTORY OF MASSACHUSETTS.

❀ We select granite for the underpinning of our houses and barns; we build fences of stone; but we do not ourselves rest on an underpinning of granite truth, the lowest primitive rock.

LIFE WITHOUT PRINCIPLE.

❀ I am sorry to think that you do not get a man's most effective criticism until you provoke him. Severe truth is expressed with some bitterness.

JOURNAL, March 15, 1854.

❀ I do not wish to flatter my townsmen, nor to be flattered by them, for that will not advance either of us. We need to be provoked—goaded like oxen, as we are, into a trot.

WALDEN, Chapter III.

❀ A world in which there is a demand for ice-creams but not for truth!

JOURNAL, August 24, 1852.

❀ Truth is ever returning into herself. I glimpse one feature today, another tomorrow; and the next day they are blended.

JOURNAL, November 13, 1837.

❀ I fear chiefly lest my expression may not be *extravagant* enough, may not wander far enough beyond the narrow limits of my daily experience, so as to be adequate to the truth of which I have been convinced.

WALDEN, Chapter XVIII.

❦ It is remarkable that among all the preachers there are so few moral teachers. The prophets are employed in excusing the ways of men.

LIFE WITHOUT PRINCIPLE.

❦ The preacher's standard of morality is no higher than that of his audience. He studies to conciliate his hearers and never to offend them.

JOURNAL, February 26, 1852.

❦ It is remarkable how long men will believe in the bottomlessness of a pond without taking the trouble to sound it.

WALDEN, Chapter XVI.

❦ You can pass your hand under the largest mob, a nation in revolution even, and, however solid a bulk they may make, like a hail-cloud in the atmosphere, you may not meet so much as a cobweb of support. They may not rest, even by a point, on eternal foundations. But an individual standing on truth you cannot pass your hand under, for his foundations reach to the center of the universe.

JOURNAL, May 4, 1852.

❦ I, too, would fain set down something beside facts. Facts should only be as the frame to my pictures; they should be material to the mythology which I am writing; not facts to assist men to make money, farmers to farm profitably, in any common sense; facts to tell who I am, and where I have been or what I have thought.

JOURNAL, November 9, 1851.

ON TRUTH

❦ Truth strikes us from behind, and in the dark, as well as from before and in broad daylight.

JOURNAL, November 5, 1837.

❦ I care not whether my vision of truth is a waking thought or dream remembered, whether it is seen in the light or in the dark. It is the subject of the vision, the truth alone, that concerns me. The philosopher for whom rainbows, etc., can be explained away never saw them.

JOURNAL, November 5, 1857.

❦ The settled lecturers are as tame as the settled ministers. The audiences do not want to hear any prophets; they do not wish to be stimulated or instructed, but entertained. They, their wives and daughters, go to the Lyceum to suck a sugar-plum. The little medicine they get is disguised with sugar. It is never the reformer they hear there, but a faint and timid echo of him only. They seek a pastime merely. Their greatest guns and sons of thunder are only wooden guns and great-grandsons of thunder, who give them smooth words well pronounced from manuscripts well punctuated—they who have stolen the little fire they have from prophets whom the audience would quake to hear. They ask for orators that will entertain them and leave them where they found them.

JOURNAL, November 16, 1858.

❦ To live in relations of truth and sincerity with men is to dwell in a frontier country.

JOURNAL, January 12, 1852.

❧ It is a great satisfaction to find that your oldest convictions are permanent. With regard to essentials, I have never had occasion to change my mind. The aspect of the world varies from year to year, as the landscape is differently clothed, but I find that the *truth* is still *true*, and I never regret any emphasis which it may have inspired.

LETTER TO HARRISON BLAKE, August 18, 1857.

❧ It is not enough that we are truthful; we must cherish and carry out high purposes to be truthful about.

LETTER TO HARRISON BLAKE, September, 1852.

On the Future of Man 🥀 🥀

🥀 If all were as it seems, and men made the elements their servants for noble ends!

WALDEN, Chapter IV.

🥀 Men have become the tools of their tools.

JOURNAL, 1845.

🥀 If we do not get out sleepers, and forge rails, and devote days and nights to the work, but go to tinkering upon our *lives* to improve *them,* who will build railroads? And if railroads are not built, how shall we get to heaven in season? But if we stay at home and mind our business, who will want railroads? We do not ride on the railroad; it rides upon us.

WALDEN, Chapter II.

⚡ Our inventions are wont to be pretty toys, which distract our attention from serious things. They are but improved means to an unimproved end, an end which it was already but too easy to arrive at; as railroads lead to Boston or New York.

WALDEN, Chapter I.

⚡ We are in great haste to construct a magnetic telegraph from Maine to Texas; but Maine and Texas, it may be, have nothing important to communicate. Either is in such a predicament as the man who was earnest to be introduced to a distinguished deaf woman, but when he was presented, and one end of her ear trumpet was put into his hand, had nothing to say. As if the main object were to talk fast and not to talk sensibly. We are eager to tunnel under the Atlantic and bring the Old World some weeks nearer to the New; but perchance the first news that will leak through into the broad, flapping American ear will be that the Princess Adelaide has the whooping cough.

WALDEN, Chapter I.

⚡ Only make something to take the place of something, and men will behave as if it was the very thing they wanted.

THE WEEK, Monday.

⚡ Almost all our improvements, so called, tend to convert the country into the town.

JOURNAL, August 22, 1860.

The whole enterprise of this nation, which is not an upward but a westward one, toward Oregon, California, Japan, etc., is totally devoid of interest to me, whether performed on foot, or by a Pacific railroad. It is not illustrated by a thought; it is not warmed by a sentiment; there is nothing in it which one should lay down his life for, nor even his gloves—hardly which one would take up a newspaper for.

LETTER TO HARRISON BLAKE, February 27, 1853.

The universe is wider than our views of it.

WALDEN, Chapter XVIII.

The only excuse for reproduction is improvement. Nature abhors repetition.

LETTER TO HARRISON BLAKE, September, 1852.

The startings and arrivals of the cars are now the epochs in the village day. They go and come with such regularity and precision, and their whistle can be heard so far, that the farmers set their clocks by them, and thus one well-constructed institution regulates a whole country. Have not men improved somewhat in punctuality since the railroad was invented? Do they not talk and think faster in the depot than they did in the stage-office?

WALDEN, Chapter IV.

Just as we are doing away with duelling or fighting one another with pistols, I think that we may in course of time do away with fighting one another with lawyers.

JOURNAL, October 22, 1859.

🖾 Where is the "unexplored land" but in our own un-tried enterprises?

LETTER TO HARRISON BLAKE, May 20, 1860.

🖾 A man is not his hope, nor his despair, nor yet his past deed. We know not yet what we have done, still less what we are doing. Wait till evening, and other parts of our day's work will shine than we had thought at noon, and we shall discover the real purport of our toil. As when the farmer has reached the end of the furrow and looks back, he can tell best where the pressed earth shines most.

THE WEEK, Monday.

🖾 Undoubtedly the very tedium and ennui which pre-sume to have exhausted the variety and the joys of life are as old as Adam. But man's capacities have never been measured; nor are we to judge of what he can do by any precedents, so little has been tried.

WALDEN, Chapter I.

🖾 While civilization has been improving our houses, it has not equally improved the men who are to inhabit them.

WALDEN, Chapter I.

🖾 Some philanthropists trust that the houses will civi-lize the inhabitants at last. The mass of men, just like savages, strive always after the outside, the clothes and finery of civilized life, the blue beads and tinsel and center-tables. It is a wonder that any load ever gets moved, men are so prone to put the cart before the horse.

JOURNAL, September 16, 1859.

ON THE FUTURE OF MAN

📚 Though it is late to leave off this wrong way, it will seem early the moment we begin in the right way; instead of mid-afternoon, it will be early morning with us. We have not got half way to dawn yet.

LETTER TO HARRISON BLAKE, April 10, 1853.

📚 I do not speak to those who are well employed, in whatever circumstances, and they know whether they are well employed or not—but mainly to the mass of men who are discontented, and idly complaining of the hardness of their lot or of the times, when they might improve them.

WALDEN, Chapter I.

📚 In a thousand apparently humble ways men busy themselves to make some right take the place of some wrong—if it is only to make a better paste blacking—and they are themselves *so much* the better morally for it.

LETTER TO HARRISON BLAKE, December 19, 1853.

📚 We survive, in one sense, in our posterity and in the continuance of our race, but when a race of men, of Indians for instance, becomes extinct, is not that the end of the world for them? Is not the world forever beginning and coming to an end, both to men and races?

JOURNAL, December 29, 1853.

📚 Heaven is under our feet as well as over our heads.

WALDEN, Chapter XVI.

📚 We do not believe that a tide rises and falls behind every man which can float the British Empire like a chip, if he should ever harbor it in its mind. Who knows what sort of seventeen-year locust will next come out of the ground? The government of the world I live in was not framed, like that of Britain, in after-dinner conversations over the wine.

WALDEN, Chapter XVIII.

To make a railroad round the world available to all mankind is equivalent to grading the whole surface of the planet. Men have an indistinct notion that if they keep up this activity of joint stocks and spades long enough all will at length ride somewhere, in next to no time, and for nothing; but though a crowd rushes to the depot, and the conductor shouts "All aboard!" when the smoke is blown away and the vapor condensed, it will be perceived that a few are riding, but the rest are run over—and it will be called, and will be, "A melancholy accident." No doubt they can ride at last who shall have earned their fare, that is, if they survive so long, but they will probably have lost their elasticity and desire to travel by that time.

WALDEN, Chapter I.

Did you ever think what those sleepers are that underlie the railroad? Each one is a man, an Irishman, or a Yankee man. The rails are laid on them, and they are covered with sand, and the cars run smoothly over them. They are sound sleepers, I assure you. And every few years a new lot is laid down and run over; so that, if some have the pleasure of riding on a rail, others have the misfortune to be ridden upon. And when they run over a man that is walking in his sleep, a supernumerary sleeper in the wrong position, and wake him up, they suddenly stop the cars, and make a hue and cry about it, as if this were an exception. I am glad to know that it takes a gang of men for every five miles to keep the sleepers down and level in their beds as it is, for this is a sign that they may sometime get up again.

WALDEN, Chapter II.

⚘ The crowd is something new, and to be attended to. It is worth a thousand Trinity Churches and Exchanges while it is looking at them, and will run over them and trample them under foot one day.

LETTER TO RALPH W. EMERSON, May 23, 1843.

⚘ It is more glorious to expect a better, than to enjoy a worse.

JOURNAL, January 26, 1852.

⚘ I never yet knew the sun to be knocked down and rolled through a mud-puddle; he comes out honor-bright from behind every storm. Let us then take sides with the sun.

LETTER TO HARRISON BLAKE, December 19, 1854.

⚘ I learned this, at least, by my experiment: that if one advances confidently in the direction of his dreams, and endeavors to live the life which he has imagined, he will meet with success unexpected in common hours. He will put some things behind, will pass an invisible boundary; new, universal, and more liberal laws will begin to establish themselves around and within him; or the old laws be expanded, and interpreted in his favor in a more liberal sense, and he will live with the license of a higher order of beings. In proportion as he simplifies his life, the laws of the universe will appear less complex, and solitude will not be solitude, nor poverty poverty, nor weakness weakness.

WALDEN, Chapter XVIII.

What was the meaning of that South-Sea Exploring Expedition, with all its parade and expense, but an indirect recognition of the fact that there are continents and seas in the moral world to which every man is an isthmus or an inlet, yet unexplored by him, but that it is easier to sail many thousand miles through cold and storm and cannibals, in a government ship, with five hundred men and boys to assist one, than it is to explore the private sea, the Atlantic and Pacific Ocean of one's being alone.

WALDEN, Chapter XVIII.

If you would learn to speak all tongues and conform to the customs of all nations, if you would travel farther than all travelers, be naturalized in all climes, and cause the Sphinx to dash her head against a stone, even obey the precept of the old philosopher, and Explore thyself. Herein are demanded the eye and the nerve. Only the defeated and deserters go to the wars, cowards that run away and enlist. Start now on that farthest western way, which does not pause at the Mississippi or the Pacific, nor conduct toward a wornout China or Japan, but leads on direct, a tangent to this sphere, summer and winter, day and night, sun down, moon down, and at last earth down too.

WALDEN, *Chapter XVIII.*

⚘ We love to fight far from home.

LETTER TO HARRISON BLAKE, December 19, 1854.

⚘ It is easier to discover another such a new world as Columbus did, than to go within one fold of this which we appear to know so well; the land is lost sight of, the compass varies, and mankind mutiny; and still history accumulates like rubbish before the portals of nature. But there is only necessary a moment's sanity and sound senses, to teach us that there is a nature behind the ordinary, in which we have only some vague preemption right and western reserve as yet. We live on the outskirts of that region. Carved wood, and floating boughs, and sunset skies are all that we know of it.

THE WEEK, Friday.

⚘ Is Franklin the only man who is lost, that his wife should be so earnest to find him? Does Mr. Grinnell know where he himself is? Be rather the Mungo Park, the Lewis and Clark and Frobisher, of your own streams and oceans; explore your own higher latitudes. Nay, be a Columbus to whole new continents and worlds within you, opening new channels, not of trade, but of thought. Every man is the lord of a realm beside which the earthly empire of the Czar is but a petty state, a hummock left by the ice. Yet some can be patriotic who have no *self*-respect, and sacrifice the greater to the less. They love the soil which makes their graves, but have no sympathy with the spirit which may still animate their clay.

WALDEN, Chapter XVIII.

Every one has heard the story which has gone the rounds of New England, of a strong and beautiful bug which came out of the dry leaf of an old table of apple-tree wood, which had stood in a farmer's kitchen for sixty years, first in Connecticut, and afterwards in Massachusetts—from an egg deposited in the living tree many years earlier still, as appeared by counting the annual layers beyond it; which was heard gnawing out for several weeks, hatched perchance by the heat of an urn. Who does not feel his faith in a resurrection and immortality strengthened by hearing of this? Who knows what beautiful and winged life, whose egg has been buried for ages under many concentric layers of woodenness in the dead dry life of society, deposited at first in the alburnum of the green and living tree, which has been gradually converted into the semblance of a well-seasoned tomb—heard perchance gnawing out now for years by the astonished family of man, as they sat round the festive board—may unexpectedly come forth from amidst society's most trivial and handselled furniture, to enjoy its perfect summer life at last!

WALDEN, Chapter XVIII.

ON THE FUTURE OF MAN

I do not say that John or Jonathan will realize all this; but such is the character of that morrow which mere lapse of time can never make to dawn. The light which puts out our eyes is darkness to us. Only that day dawns to which we are awake. There is more day to dawn. The sun is but a morning star.

WALDEN, Chapter XVIII.